Being and

Volume C
Peak Oil Philosophy and the Ontology of Limitation

Chad A. Haag
Uchakkada, India
2019

# Table of Contents
## Volume One

Dedicated to ........................................................................................... 4

Part I .................................................................................................... 6

  Chapter One: The Coming of Peak Oil Philosophy ......................... 8

  Chapter Two: The Bastard in the Court ........................................ 77

    Part II ........................................................................................ 89

    Being ......................................................................................... 89

    Chapter Three: ......................................................................... 91

    Dialectic and Hierarchy: ........................................................... 91

    Hegelian Negation and Haagian Limitation ............................. 91

    Chapter Four .......................................................................... 129

  Peak Oil and Existentialist Finitude: ............................................ 129

    Against German Idealism and Dialectical Materialism
.................................................................................................. 129

    Part III ..................................................................................... 169

    Truth ....................................................................................... 169

    Chapter Five ........................................................................... 171

    Apocalypsed Not: ................................................................... 171

    The Crisis of Manifestation in the Twilight of Fossil
Fuels ........................................................................................ 171

Dedicated to
the three great truth-bearing prophets of our era:
Alan Collinge, student loan justice fighter;
John Michael Greer, Peak Oil green wizard;
And Ted Kaczynski, anti-technological industrialism martyr;
Also, to the community of anti-academic independent intellectuals,
the viewers of the chadafrican channel;
Finally, to my wife Minu V, with love.
Uchakkada, India
16-01-2019

"Her worst oppressor had been a man the world called civilized" — Robert E. Howard, *Iron Shadows in the Moon,* from *The Coming of Conan the Cimmerian*

"Our entire economy has assumed the characteristics of a bubble or Ponzi scheme" — Richard Heinberg, *The End of Growth*

"Thou shalt not make a machine in the likeness of a human mind" — Frank Herbert, *Dune*

"The technophiles are taking us all on an utterly reckless ride into the unknown. Many people understand something of what technological progress is doing to us yet take a passive attitude toward it because they think it is inevitable. But we (FC) don't think it is inevitable. We think it can be stopped" — Ted Kaczynski, *Industrial Society and Its Future*

"The decades to come will see many things that are now done by machines handed back over to human beings" — John Michael Greer, "After the Prosthetic Society"

"If you are a man, Winston, you are the last man. Your kind is extinct" — George Orwell, *1984*

# Part I
# Oil

"As soon as what is unconcealed no longer concerns man even as object, but does so, rather, exclusively as standing-reserve, and man in the midst of objectlessness is nothing but the orderer of the standing-reserve, then he comes to the very brink of a precipitous fall; that is, he comes to the point where he himself will have to be taken as standing-reserve. Meanwhile, man precisely as the one so threatened, exalts himself to the posture of lord of the earth" — Martin Heidegger, "The Question Concerning Technology"

# Chapter One
## "The Coming of Peak Oil" Philosophy

### A Peak Oil Philosophy Manifesto

In this text is attempted the venture of providing the first ever book-length manifesto of Peak Oil Philosophy. Such a book is as necessary as it is unprecedented, given that Peak Oil is neither a mere "theory" from the fringes of the conspiracy movement nor a "problem of geology" best left to a handful of scientists whose salaries from academic, industrial, and government sources will surely distort their research to fit a certain pre-determined bias favouring more petroleum consumption, even as the demonstrable fact that the globe has already surpassed the peak of Hubbert's Curve of depletion in 2005 has manifested itself in waves of economic dysfunction, political deadlock, and geopolitical instability ever since. Such easy dismissals of the very concept of pursuing a Peak Oil Philosophy could only proceed by suggesting, *preposterously*, that living in an age dominated by the burning of vast amounts of fossil fuels somehow would not indicate that those fuels held some central, foundational role in sustaining the very fabric of the world of mythological meanings which make up the default horizon for those who have not yet been "given the sunglasses" to see the aliens behind the smiling faces, the true messages behind the advertisement billboards, and the immense power of petroleum behind the "accomplishments" so loudly and self-righteously trumpeted by the media.

Even the achievement of the internet, the most beloved of all recent feats, cannot honestly be described as anything except a secondary side effect of burning vast amounts of fossil fuels. The popular mythology that celebrates the CEOs profiting from the Technology Industry as modern-day geniuses with intellects far surpassing the classical geniuses like Isaac Newton and Galileo betrays an astonishing confusion among an energy source, a machine that burns it, and a corporate asshole who profits from the burning of that energy, without which his sacred algorithm and its fiercely-guarded "intellectual property rights" patents would dissolve into so much worthless abstraction unfit even to be run in the ideal privacy of one's own mind. The myth that Mark Zuckerberg's "genius" is somehow the "efficient cause" behind a globally-distributed network of machines that allow users to share status updates with content as "important" as a photo of the chalupa combo they grabbed at Taco Bell on their lunch break can only make sense if we assume that Zuckerberg were really crunching all those numbers in his brain to process the data for two billion FaceMash users. When confronted with the enormous power of the worldwide web, we make a grave error by mistaking the vast inputs of electrical energy which powers all of those machines for the "power of the intellect" of some CEO who is merely a tiny financial parasite on the giant beast of fossil fuel power. The 23,200 hours of human labour contained in just one barrel of oil is intrinsically a sublime amount of energy; yet in modern contexts, this would barely cover the energy requirements for a single day's commutes for all of some Silicon Valley campus's "environmentalist" corporate employees' SUV's (complete with their "certified tree hugger" bumper stickers) to their politically correct campus layered with photo-op-ready solar panels, as though layering a few solar panels on the roof could even *begin* to offset the enormous environmental damage which the industry commits on a daily basis from precisely the most politically correct area of the nation where voicing nominal concern over Climate Change is an entrenched but meaningless factor of the social code. One could only imagine how many hours of human labour are wasted each day to feed the world's army of mammoth data centres, a storage of raw fossil fuel horsepower which somehow gets misrecognized as the internal workings of some corporate CEO's "brilliance." Considering that some 1/5 of global electricity use is projected to be consumed by data centres by the year 2025, the number is vast enough to become intuitively meaningless.

    The strangest thing about such a scenario is that the most honest answer to the question of the essence of the internet is also the most invisible to the media and technological aristocracy of CEOs who profit enormously from burning unspeakably vast reserves of an energy source which somehow still remains invisible to them. Obsessions over intellectual property rights, marketing strategies, stock values, business loans, and demographic niches all miss the point that every one of these corporate boardroom concerns is merely a secondary and incomplete euphemism for talking about the same, single substance, without which each of these would dissolve into nothingness: *everything we do is just a euphemism for burning fossil fuels.*

Few terms are as demonized in Modern Philosophy as "dualism," yet the dualism between a crucial energy resource and the many ways of burning it out of existence reveals that it is not only our most-celebrated objective accomplishments, such as the internet, that crumble into contingency when revealed to be nothing more than secondary effects of living in an era of fossil fuels: our very structure of subjectivity is similarly reduced to a euphemism for the overwhelming presence of fossil fuels. This presence is so pervasive that we risk not even seeing the fossil fuel elephant in the room as a definite object, since "seeing fossil fuels" has come to be the very transcendental shape by which any other object, even an empirical barrel of oil in the flesh, must be appropriated. Petroleum's historical contingency confirms rather than negates this principle, as it is only one of several crucial resources which have transcended empirical objectivity to effect a transcendental re-standardization of consciousness. A woolly mammoth hunter from the Ice Age would "see mammoths" (as the form of a levelled-out relation to Nature as a pseudo-social animistic force rather than raw matter to be processed industrially) even if an empirical mammoth did not come to occupy his frame of sight at that moment, just as an Ancient Egyptian agricultural peasant would "see grain" (as the circular form of processes that cycle through repeating phases in order to flesh out a pre-given tendency towards completion) even if an empirical field of barley were not literally occupying his frame of sight at that moment. We also fail to see "fossil fuels" as an object pervading our civilization because we are always already "seeing fossil fuels" as our transcendental frame of intuition, a frame with a level of abstraction so refined that even a laymen who never sees a physical barrel of empirical petroleum even once in his life will still spend his entire life in modernity "seeing fossil fuels" through forcing every other objective content to conform to the shape of surplus and explosive growth, a conceptual schema into which even a real barrel of oil in the flesh must fit in order to be intelligible.

Petroleum's dominance over our modern way of thinking is best evidenced by precisely those acts of thinking which explicitly reject the pollution and alienation of Fossil Fuel Modernity at the surface level of appearance but portray even the post-apocalyptic future devastated by ecological crisis as still transcendentally-structured by the shape of Fossil Fuels. David Klass's novel *Firestorm* centres around a boy who had been sent from a thousand years in the future back to our time to warn us about the apocalyptic scale of environmental damage which will have devastated the Earth by his era, with the hope that this warning might awaken the readers in the early 21st Century to support ecologically-sensitive responses to prevent such a future from materializing. The boy is pursued by evil figures who follow him from the future and try to kill him off before he can spread his ecological message to the masses. It is truly bizarre, however, that these figures try to kill him with ray guns and other Science Fiction weapons which have not even been invented yet, as though even in a future ravaged by environmental destruction, technological progress would still continue into the next *millennium* undisturbed. In addition, the presence of a time machine capable of teleporting both the boy and his would-be killers from the future implies that a device far too sophisticated to be invented even now at the height of Fossil Fuel Modernity would somehow be available in a dystopian future ravaged by poverty and violence.[1] At the same time, Klass certainly *doesn't* suggest that this technological progress would stop even in the Green Future the readers are persuaded to pursue, even though sacrificing most of the Modern Technology today would be the only action that could make a significant difference. Klass's novel is perhaps the best testament to how pervasive fossil fuels' influence on our thinking has become, in that even our conscious attempts to

---

[1] Klass, David, *Firestorm* (New York: France Foster Books, 2008).

warn against Fossil Fuel Industrialism still assume that it will continue for centuries into the future. It is literally easier to imagine the end of the world than to imagine the end of technological progress. Even a book explicitly written to halt burning too much oil is still incomprehensible outside a type of transcendental filter which distorts contents to fit the petroleum-based shape of surplus and explosive growth even into the most ghastly of futures.

Likewise, the present volume will be built around the outrageous claim that empirical oil is not transcendental oil. If one were to somehow collect all the extant barrels of empirical petroleum left on the earth and add them up, the sum total would still be less than a single frame of transcendental Petroleum lodged deep within one subject's mind. The counter-mathematics whereby $(a + b + c + d \ldots ) < 1$ will likely offend the rationalist sensibilities of philosophers as much as it will offend the practical sensibilities of Peak Oil collapse-preppers: yet such a Copernican shift from oil as so much material stuff in a gas tank to Oil as an abstract schema into which even this "real stuff" must pass, in a bizarre act of self-recursive bootstrapping, in order to make sense is precisely what will be required to move beyond the non-action and false-stops which have paralyzed humanity in its response to the decline of industrialism. Transcendental oil is the limit of empirical oil, the excess which remains even after every extant barrel of empirical oil has been collected but a mysterious limit remains unaccounted for. This distinction between empirical and transcendental oil is evidenced by the way that in the pre-fossil fuel era oil certainly was known by humans, but it was largely seen as a waste product or perhaps just a substitute for whale blubber, since the standard by which it was evaluated was agrarian grain. Paradoxically, even oil cannot be itself without passing through the transcendental filter which it self-recursively generates itself.

Thus, the difference between an Ice Age hunter gatherer, an Ancient Egyptian agrarian peasant, and a modern day fossil fuel-based social media user amounts to far more than a difference in numerical coordinates on the abstract timeline of historical evolution; it would be wrong to assume that the same phenomenological structure of human subjectivity has been preserved unchanged in this straight line of succession from "primitive man" to "modern man," such that all throughout history humans were merely awaiting the moment of liberation in which they could finally embody the "normal lifestyle" of a suburban couch potato which had been one's "intrinsic human nature" all along. Under this view one could only wonder how Ancient Assyrian pagan astrologers and Medieval Norse blacksmiths ever managed to survive without having spent a single day "realizing their True Human Nature," since both passed their entire lives without ever watching a sitcom on television and without ever sharing a photo with 900 of their closest friends on FaceMash in order to closely watch the "like meter" bid up that photo's stock value and administer a hit of dopamine to the "social media like junkie" who has effectively become dopamine-impotent without the extra help which his or her smartphone provides. It is not an exaggeration to say that excessive social media mediation of pleasure may have rendered an entire generation incapable of "feeling it" without the detour which that person's phone provides by sending him or her digital commands with the message "Feel pleasure!" The social media notification panel has become something of a purely abstract pornography, the raw command to "feel good" stripped of any specific content as such, but without which the individual is rendered numb to even enjoy a night out with friends in the real world until someone comes along to like the status update containing photos and a tagged location for the event. A mere three days later, of course, the same digital photo will have been completely forgotten and each of those likes rendered utterly worthless as the user will have already jumped back onto the hamster wheel of social media attention seeking with another half-dozen selfies.

    Yet dwelling on FaceMash betrays the author's age, as the pace of (nominal) change is so rapid that many of the technological fads currently sweeping the youth include gimmicks which the author admittedly could not even name. Yet even though the media praises each of these as some radical innovation "never thought of before," it would be hard to argue that sharing short video clips of oneself set to music represents anything which could not have been accomplished with a camcorder and VCR in an era before smartphones had even been considered. On a more fundamental level, it would seem strange to argue that millions of years of human evolution has merely awaited the moment that Tik Tok could provide an objective form which would symmetrically fit some eternal subjective structure which had awaited all those millennia to find realization.

In contrast with such a preposterous claim, the author shall argue that the very transcendental horizon of subjective meaningfulness underwent a radical shift in the movement from hunter gatherer to agrarian to fossil fuel-based worldviews and is undergoing another similar shift as the author writes these words; the very epistemological foundation of consciousness holds a different and irreconcilable shape at each level which cannot be carried over to the next level without sacrificing its geometrical integrity in order to give way to the next worldview. The transition to the fossil fuel worldview was not an irreversible accomplishment to "fulfil Mankind's historical destiny," as the folk mythology of progress claims. Rather, as the very material basis of this worldview is being burned out of existence in countless tailpipes and smokestacks around the industrialized world, another change of resource base will inevitably bring about the destruction of this worldview and clear the path for a transition to another shape of consciousness to take its place. This process will not merely transform one's subjective frame of perception, leaving the world of meanings, objects, systems, and mythologies intact. Rather, the very world we inhabit, insofar as it simply is a world upheld by the substance of fossil fuels, will collapse into nothingness and worthless illusion as the tectonic plates of historical change shift, birthing a radically new post-oil world into existence. This destruction of the very fabric of our worldview will not just entail an exhaustive concatenation of every fact or attitude to be marched one by one to the execution chamber of historical decline; above all, the very shape by which meaning is generated in the future will be transformed from the expectation that contents conform to the geometrical metaphor of "progress" to an expectation favouring a totally different geometrical metaphor. This transition will be the subject of the present volume.

*Peak Oil Literature and the Problem of Terminology*

The present text represents a revolutionary departure from the way that Peak Oil Literature has traditionally been carried out, given that no Peak Oil book written thus far has ever simultaneously attempted to launch a full-scale, systematic critique of Fundamental Ontology in the spirit of figures like Martin Heidegger, Alain Badiou, or Slavoj Zizek. Although no Peak Oil Ontology has ever yet been attempted as such, the author argues that no honest analysis of Peak Oil has ever managed to fully avoid the ontological problem of Being. Interestingly, despite lacking any explicitly-fixed protocols determining the "right words" by which to describe the relation between a sprawling world of illusory social constructs and the fossil fuel resource base underlying it, writers as different as John Michael Greer, James Howard Kunstler, Richard Heinberg, Dmitry Orlov, and Michael Rupert have all formulated their theses around this dualistic, hierarchical relation in which, clearly, the fossil fuel resource base is just far more *real* than the system of surface appearances of modernity which float over this underlying base like so much froth on the top of a dark, well-brewed mug of oatmeal stout pulled from the basement brewery of some faithful adherent to Greer's favourite bit of *Green Wizardry* advice.[2]

Virtually every piece of literature written in the Peak Oil genre has been structured around the same challenge: how can one describe a dualistic hierarchy between oil and surface appearances? This challenge is compounded by the fact that this dualism is as invisible to those outside the Peak Oil Community as the aliens

---

[2] In *Green Wizardry* Greer recommends relocating to a house with "a basement where you can get to work learning to brew good beer." Such a hypothetical green wizard brewer who follows this advice would be well-prepared to greet the Four Horsemen of Apocalypse with a cold one when they arrive at the door on queue with the collapse of industrial civilization. See Greer, John Michael, *Green Wizardry* (Gabriola Island: New Society Publishers, 2013), Kindle Locations 3099-3100.

were to those who lacked the sunglasses in the classic film *They Live*. *They Live*, of course, famously portrayed an intergalactic conspiracy in which a mysterious pair of sunglasses enabled a man to see that below the surface of smiling "everymen" in business suits lay monstrous, skeletal faces and behind innocuous billboards promoting a beloved product's brand lay the raw, sinister commands "Obey! Consume! Stay Asleep!" As Zizek noted, the sunglasses in *They Live* provide something of a direct short-circuit that allows one to "see ideology" in its purified form.[3] The experience of undergoing initiation into the Peak Oil Community can quite legitimately be compared to obtaining a pair of sunglasses that allow one to penetrate beyond the fleeting world of surface appearances, but rather than find a flurry of ideological messages spelled out linguistically in phrases like "Obey!" and "Watch TV!" and rather than find a plurality of malicious alien faces hidden within the human population like so many of David Icke's reptilian lizards, the new recruit into the world of Peak Oil is dazzled by the simplicity and singularity of what he or she finds, everywhere, under the surface of our experiences: *behind everything, there is nothing but oil.*

Peak Oil Philosophy's ontological challenge therefore lies in explaining that if nothing has *more* Being than oil, then even our systems of thought, linguistic messages of meaning, mythologies of personal self-description, and political ideologies do not have "no being at all" so much as they only have being insofar as they transitively borrow a certain portion of Being from oil, a donation from this sublimely-powerful source which will always still be *less* than the massive reservoir of Being from which it was borrowed. Any student familiar with the History of Western Philosophy may immediately be at a loss for how to describe this peculiar arrangement between borrower of Being and borrowed Being with the resources available from the established systems of Ontology. Such a search will go on in vain as no established philosophy is satisfactorily suited to meet this unique and puzzling task. For this reason, the present volume will formulate a unique ontology from

---

[3] Zizek, Slavoj, *The Ticklish Subject* (London: Verso, 2000), p. 54.

the fertile soil of serious confrontation with the problem of Peak Oil rather than conform to the pressures of academic fashionableness to adopt some system of sophistry from Deconstruction or Psychoanalysis, systems of pure abstraction which would only construct a room full of mirrors beyond which a real world burning through its last reserves of fossil fuels would fail to shrine through.

Each of the four earliest great Peak Oil writers tended to employ his own favourite term to describe this relation between oil and the surface world of appearances. Michael Ruppert, one of the earliest thinkers to write seriously on the topic before his tragic death in 2014, tended to favour emphasizing that our entire world of consumer products, almost without exception, is quite literally "made of it." In his classic *Crossing the Rubicon: The Decline of American Empire and the End of the Age of Oil*, he enumerates a list of ordinary products which are all just so many ways of repackaging oil into a seemingly different object without ever departing from the same substance:

> Oil pervades our civilization; it is all around you. The shell for your computer is made from it. Your food comes wrapped in it. You brush your hair and teeth with it. There's probably some in your shampoo, and most certainly some in its container. Your children's toys are made from it. You take your trash out in it. It makes your clothes soft in the dryer. As you change the channels with the TV remote you hold it in your hands. Some of your furniture is probably made with it. It is everywhere inside your car. It is used in both the asphalt you drive on and the tires that meet the road . . . Oh yes, and the healthy water you carry around with you comes packaged in it.[4]

As the list expands to encompass virtually every item in one's *Lebenswelt*, Ruppert addresses the reader's predictable unease by warning that even if he or she becomes disturbed enough by these revelations to react by throwing the book away, he or she will just

---

[4] Ruppert, Michael. *Crossing the Rubicon* (Gabriola Island: New Society Publishers, 2004), pp.23-24.

confirm the irony of the situation by throwing the book into a trashcan which is also "made from it."

Much of Ruppert's argument in *Crossing the Rubicon* consisted in detailing the extent to which the United States and its allies began making preparations for a series of resource wars in the Middle East (Iraq) and Central Asia (Afghanistan) during the 1990's (long before September 11, 2001) when the looming problem of Peak Oil began to silently influence geopolitical decisions behind the elites' closed doors, despite the media's continued refusal to even utter the word "Peak Oil." Ruppert's emphasis on oil as the material cause of our modern world naturally implied that it was the struggle over possession of this precious material which motivated the coordinated and deeply unethical conspiracy to launch a series of resource wars which continue to the present day.

Michael Ruppert emphasized the shocking fact that at this point in history, the "material cause" behind nearly every consumer product is just oil and that the struggle to acquire a steady supply of this material motivated the ghastly foreign policy decisions of both the Clinton and Bush administrations. Richard Heinberg differed slightly from Ruppert by emphasizing oil's role as something like an efficient cause generating the sprawling world of modernity as a secondary result of burning fossil fuels. Heinberg notes that the complexity so celebrated in our era is not the result of human intelligence so much as it is a side effect of using fossil fuels which were inaccessible to pre-modern eras: "We also tend to see the unprecedented levels of complexity of our society today as resulting from the historically recent energy subsidies of fossil fuels."[5] Heinberg's 2011 work *The End of Growth: Adapting to Our New Economic Reality* expanded this insight into an impressively-thorough book-length critique of the very notion that "economic growth" can be a reasonable long-term goal if "economic growth" literally amounts to nothing more than a secondary side effect generated from the agency of fossil fuel resources, resources which

---

[5] Heinberg, Richard, "Conflict in the Era of Economic Decline" In *Afterburn: Society Beyond Fossil Fuels* (Gabriola Island: New Society Publishers, 2015), p. 117.

have already begun to decline.[6] In the absence of petroleum and other fossil fuels which act as the unstated "efficient cause" behind economic growth, no amount of financial, scientific, technological, or political tinkering can restore the fundamental "first mover" which fossil fuels had provided in the background all along.

James Howard Kunstler can be considered to continue the Aristotelian enumeration through the four causes by complementing these two approaches with his own tendency to expose the utter stupidity and short-sightedness of suburban sprawl, a project he routinely calls the single greatest misinvestment of resources in Human History:

> Since suburbia had to be understood by definition as a way of life with no future, all that activity [of building strip malls, giant retail centres, and armies of SUV's to complement the uniquely dysfunctional geography of suburban sprawl] represented a massive misinvestment in [even] more stuff with no future. How tragic was that?[7]

The power of fossil fuels was so concentrated and so enormous that we could have effectively done *anything* with the incredible power they temporarily gave us; yet what we did with them was build suburbs. Worse still, these suburbs were so poorly constructed that they will only be semi-viable for a short few decades of Human History.[8] Even while they are still standing, they provide an

---

[6] Heinberg, Richard, *The End of Growth: Adapting to Our New Economic Reality* (Gabriola Island: New Society Publishers, 2011).
[7] Kunstler, James Howard. *Too Much Magic: Wishful Thinking, Technology, and the Fate of the Nation* (New York: Grove Press, 2012).

[8] Dmitry Orlov has correctly described the well-marketed but shoddily-constructed suburban trash which provided the wildly-overpriced material for the Housing Bubble in the United States as follows: "By a lucky accident, much of the suburban housing stock is actually of very low intrinsic value, constructed out of a few sticks, a bit of tarpaper and some plastic and cardboard sheets. These American-style Potemkin villages will be simple to knock down . . . the merest touch from a bulldozer will be sufficient to cause these little market bubbles to fold up into a pile of of kindle and dust with barely a groan."

environment that is so boring and so unsatisfying to live in that suicidal ideation is a routinely-reported outcome of spending one's entire existence in the cardboard prison cell which one of these half million-dollar McMansions amounts to in reality. It would be difficult to imagine the historically-anomalous Emo Movement without suburbs, since "being depressed within suburbia" (or, in many cases, "being so bored that you'll pretend to be depressed just to have something to do") literally became a "common interest" around which a high school clique formed, right alongside such activities as playing football, skateboarding, or attending rodeos. If nothing else, one certainly *should* be depressed by the unimaginably vast reserves of fossil fuel resources that were dumped into the futile project of constructing an enormous, coast-to-coast suburban infrastructure which will shortly become utterly worthless, unusable trash when 90 minute commutes from home to the office become a bad memory from the past. This squandering of precious non-renewable resources for the construction of short-lived, not to mention just plain *ugly*, suburbs could only be justified by the assumption that fossil fuels were the unstated teleological cause providing the rationale for an activity that would amount to sheer insanity otherwise. The teleological goal of driving an SUV 160 miles per day over freeways suffocated with stagnant traffic and lined with miles of redundant strip-malls and vast parking lots completely devoid of aesthetic beauty cannot be subordinated to any aim or purpose except the circular, self-enclosed loop of "doing activities that burn fossil fuels in order to do activities that burn fossil fuels." Economic growth may have at one time been measured by metrics as meaningful as agricultural prosperity or the production of tangible goods; in more recent years, "economic prosperity" is literally just a measure for how rapidly and how irresponsibly we can burn fossil fuels for no goal except to burn fossil fuels.

    John Michael Greer, the greatest of the Peak Oil authors, closes the Aristotelian loop of causes by providing the most mysterious and the most compelling of the four by arguing that the

---

*Reinventing Collapse: The Soviet Experience and American Prospects* (Gabriola Island: New Society Publishers, 2011)

social constructs populating the surface level "above" petroleum cannot be properly understood unless one realizes that they do not only have oil as their efficient cause, as Heinberg emphasized; they also have the same rational "shape" as oil. Isolating the formal cause of oil will serve as a universal skeleton key to unlock the secrets of phenomena as distantly-related as the political ideologies, religious creeds, and mythological narratives of modernity. The Religion of Progress, for example, is not just a side effect of petroleum; it is the shape of petroleum, or more precisely the shape of explosive growth and guaranteed surplus, mapped into the spiritual realm of Religion.

Not coincidentally, Aristotle also prioritized formal cause over the other three causes by arguing that the key to Essence lay in properly grasping an object's form in intuition. Essence is not a linguistic definition built up from "the right words," nor is it to be satisfactorily answered by asking the material cause question "What is it made of?"; the efficient cause question "What set it into motion?"; or even the teleological cause question "What purpose will this serve?" Although all four are legitimate explanations for what something is, the most important of the four is the form. It would be difficult, for example, if given the efficient cause of a blacksmith, the teleological cause of war, and the material cause of iron to know whether one was speaking about a battle axe, a dagger, or a spearhead. If one grasped the form, even in the absence of words, one could easily distinguish one of these from the others.

One could argue that, even without an explicitly-Aristotelian motivation to do so, Greer succeeded in isolating this most important key to the Essence of Fossil Fuels by similarly recognizing the peculiar and historically-unprecedented tendency for modern mythologies, religious doctrines, systems of meaning, and expectations about history to be retrofitted to a new shape after the dawn of Fossil Fuels. In a certain sense, the shape of recent history is accurately captured by the geometrical representation of an ascending ray of progress, in which the explosive power of fossil fuels relative to past energy sources like medieval agrarian grain and Ice Age herds of woolly mammoths provided a temporary surplus of energy that allowed humanity to "progress" from agrarian economies powered by horses and hand tools to modern industrial economies powered by a vast network of machines fuelled by petroleum, natural gas, and coal. Our intuition of this shape of progress, though, has fed into a faith that Progress will never end, a faith which a priori rules out any other shapes of meaning that deviate from the model of infinite, linear ascension. Although circular models of historical repetition and bell curve-shaped models of decline that posit the era of fossil fuels as a short-lived historical anomaly which will never repeat are far more likely to fit the facts of the future than this irrational belief in infinite progress, these shapes are literally unthinkable for those uninitiated into the Peak Oil Worldview.

    Thus, Greer differed from other collapse theorists by suggesting that the biggest challenge in confronting Peak Oil does not lie in gathering the right statistical data or engineering a bulletproof rational transition plan, but rather in exposing that the mythology of progress is just the essence of fossil fuels translated into the epistemological medium of an emotionally-compelling narrative. Although it would require a full book of its own to examine more than a tiny handful of Greer's many philosophical insights on Peak Oil, one of his most memorable philosophical theories is his recognition that Mythology is the default epistemological structure of human thought. The phrase "thinking with myths" is, as he is fond of repeating, as redundant as the phrase "walking with feet."[9] If you are thinking, in other words, you are already by default using mythology to do so. While traditional tribal cultures trafficked in a number of different myths in order to provide a type of epistemological flexibility in the face of a diverse range of real-life situations, the modern Western psyche has shrunk down to a single myth sufficient to explain, supposedly, "any problem." That myth is, of course, the narrative in which Progress has already led humans from the caves to the suburbs but will continue leading us to the stars, provided that someone from the preferred political party of the person telling the myth is only allowed another term in office.

---

[9] Greer, John Michael, "Knowing Only One Story," in *The Archdruid Report*, Vol. 1 (Chicago: Founders House, 2017), p. 14.

For the early Greer, any human thought, however seemingly "scientific" or "objective," presupposes some underlying narratological pathway which provides an implicit sequence of events leading from conflict to resolution. Myths help the subject to understand the cosmos by fitting him or her into a character role within a story. The myth therefore provides "meaning" to life both in the figurative sense of spiritual valence and in the literal sense of epistemological intelligibility. This mythological horizon of meaning extends even to activities otherwise thought to be purely objective. Science, for example, never takes place in a vacuum of "disinterested pursuit of the truth." Scientists conduct their research with the implicit understanding that they are working to further mankind beyond the ignorance of the pre-scientific past by providing knowledge which will later find some engineering application to raise standards of living or improve public health. What they too often fail to see is that the recent rise in standards of living and improvements in public health did not primarily occur as the result of deducing obscure truths from arcane sub-sub-fields of Natural Science, virtually all of which would be disproven and rendered obsolete just a little bit later by someone else. The nominal improvement in standard of living and public health were primarily just the side effect of burning vast amounts of fossil fuels; without this crucial energy subsidy, the scientific knowledge itself would devolve into intellectual curiosities restricted to the paper medium of the inside of a textbook or journal article. The unspoken truth about the public's support (both emotionally and financially) for the sciences lies in the implicit agreement that all of this research will find its way into some tangible benefit to the public. Few things are as heretical as pointing out, however, that much of this loudly-trumpeted research in recent years has ended up generating toxic waste which poisoned water sources, poorly-understood drugs with nasty side effects that were only discovered *after* the patient provided living collateral damage to the experiment, risky surgical procedures resulting in countless deaths, and armies of machines that have put skilled tradespeople out of work and therefore made them too poor to afford the skyrocketing medical costs in the first place. The public's support for the sciences should not be misconstrued as some disinterested subsidy to "knowledge for knowledge's sake," however piously such a creed might be publicly professed. The understanding that mutual benefit should be the outcome of this deal is beginning to break down as we speak, though far more people think this privately than are willing to say it publicly.

At any rate, without extravagant inputs from fossil fuels, much of this scientific research will either become useless to put to industrial use or impossible to conduct in the first place. Already, each new major scientific discovery requires a larger investment of energy and financial resources, a process that is not far away from reaching the point of diminishing returns, if it has not already done so. The $13.25 billion dollars that were required to discover the Higgs boson demonstrate the financial unsustainability of continuing this project for very much longer into an era in the near future when the majority of people will find trouble meeting much more immediate needs such as finding enough food, shelter, and potable water to survive within a declining society no longer able to skate by on stealing unearned stored labour from fossil fuels. Historians of the far future will likely portray the 20th and early 21st Centuries as anomalous periods, defined by a myopic fixation on dumping outrageous sums of money into super-specialized research that progressively became ever costlier to pursue and ever less beneficial to the public until the funds and energy sources finally ran dry and paved the way for a crash into an intellectual Dark Age from which the sciences did not even begin to make a comeback from until a few centuries later.

Greer's tendency to fit rational problem solving (even including the most prestigious of modern sciences) into its role as a minor actor in a broader mythological narrative of progress with no intrinsic relation to Science has allowed him to point out that solving the gnostic puzzle of crunching the right numbers to find a rationally-viable technical solution to Peak Oil will inevitably fail if it does not penetrate to the deep mythological layer that minimally structures expectations about the present in terms of a presumed narratological path to the future, a path the validity of which stems far more from hijacking the deep spiritual layer of human motivation than relying on the much more fragile realm of abstract logical consistency. If the reader harbours any doubt about the sufficiency of a purely theoretical plan to solve the challenge of Peak Oil without first addressing the Myth of Progress, he or she could consider that of the countless rational plans that have been proposed to "smoothly transition" to a post-Peak world, not even *one* has ever been put into practice.[10]

Likewise, the essence of the Age of Oil is not to be found in isolating the material cause of petroleum's chemical makeup, such as some variation on the prototype $C_nH_{2n+2}$. Many of the petroleum engineers who have the best understanding of this material cause aspect arguably have the poorest understanding of petroleum's formal distortion of their own mythology to fit a shape of infinite progress. Most of the scientists and engineers who think they know oil when they see it fail to recognize it in their own thinking, since their irrational expectation for infinite economic and technological progress is simply the formal essence of petroleum mapped onto the abstract medium of human cognition. After all, that which explosively returns a vast surplus of energy relative to a modest investment into discovery and extraction costs simply *is* the essence of petroleum. Its economic track record of lifting agrarian societies into industrialism was just this formal essence of rapid, exponential growth mapped onto the temporal medium of history.

This formal essence's migration from physical petroleum to the abstract realm of the mind is not as controversial as it might seem. Aristotle already realized millennia ago that formal essence can quite easily be abstracted from the material cause of the substance in which it inheres. In fact, Aristotle argued that understanding occurs precisely by those means. One has only really accomplished the task of understanding an essence if one has grasped the essence in its formal purity and subtracted the material which it accidentally inhabited. To use Aristotle's own favourite

---

[10] In a memorable blog post from 2007, Greer mentioned that he was personally receiving rational plans to save the Earth from Peak Oil about once per month. To this day, not a single one of them has ever made it past the planning phase. Greer, John Michael, "The Failure of Reason" in *The Archdruid Report* Vol. 1 (Chicago: Founders House, 2017), p. 156.

example, a ring's shape can be abstracted from the material of gold to leave both a goldless imprint in a piece of wax and a similar goldless imprint in the human mind which captures the essence precisely by subtracting its material makeup from its intuitively-graspable form. On the other hand, grasping the element of gold (Au) would be quite useless if one failed to grasp its shape as a ring.[11] This archaic theory finds unexpected confirmation in Oil's formal essence's ability to be easily abstracted from its material makeup of $C_nH_{2n+2}$ to distort the epistemological medium of mythological thought or the temporal medium of historical change.

The chief barrier to grasping the seriousness of Peak Oil similarly does not lie in an improper understanding of the chemistry of petroleum, since the professional geologists and engineers employed by industry are arguably the most competent at understanding that material aspect while remaining completely blind to how dependent their own mythology of progress is to the formal essence of the petroleum reserves which are quickly being burned out of existence by their own industrial activity. Likewise, the author agrees with Greer that although all four causes are extremely important, the philosophical problem of Peak Oil must prioritize this formal essence which virally migrates from petroleum as such to the abstract realms of mythology, history, and cognition in general to infect each new host with a formal distortion to which the victim quickly becomes completely blind, because the *only* thing they can see afterwards is this shape.

*Beyond Mythology: Nietzsche, Peterson, and Greer*

It can be granted that thinkers as diverse as John Michael Greer, Jordan Peterson, and Friedrich Nietzsche agree that the mythological horizon (or for Nietzsche, simply the aesthetic) is the default standpoint from which meanings are primordially disclosed. Following this logic, deviating away from mythology requires an explicit act of abstraction. Still, there is great disagreement about what exactly this other frame of meaning is which one achieves

---

[11] Aristotle, *De Anima*, in *Basic Works of Aristotle* (New York: the Modern Library, 2001), p. 580.

after breaking from myth. Greer's stance, of course, is that our contemporary Mythology of Progress is just a euphemism for really talking about the fossil fuels which enable every aspect of our historically anomalous and deeply wasteful lifestyles, a stance with which the author does not disagree. Nietzsche differed from this clean dualism between myth and "real object" by rejecting all dualisms: there is no other horizon really "beyond" which would be more substantial and more firmly grounded in some archaic dualistic sense. All one will find by suspending the aesthetic appreciation of life is the nihilistic groundlessness of a set of meanings with no further guarantee beyond themselves. The supreme act of the Will to Power would be to affirm these groundless values and life-images simply on the basis of their aesthetic beauty, knowing that this aesthetic attitude is not simply an impoverished version of the theoretical quest for Truth once favoured in Classical Philosophy.[12] The early Jordan Peterson's stance, as something of a psychological "scientist" is far less sceptical: consciously suspending a mythological "significance" that has long been taken for granted as meaningful in order to achieve a scientifically-purified account of the "consensually validatable properties" of an object stripped of its cultural meaningfulness is not a confrontation with nothingness, as Nietzsche would claim: it is the very gateway to transforming cultural significance into a scientific essence.[13] In *Maps of Meaning*, Peterson himself gives the example of the sun: long considered a mythological deity with consciousness and volition, the subtraction of all mythical significance eventually yielded the scientifically-objective essence of the sun now known to astronomers.[14] What one finds beyond mythology, for Peterson, is just a set of all the essences knowable by science.

Likewise, all three believed that there are no more than two layers of meaning which can be traversed. Greer held a dualism between fossil fuels and the myth of progress. Nietzsche affirmed

---

[12] Nietzsche, Friedrich, *The Gay Science*, in *The Delphi Complete Works of Friedrich Nietzsche* (Kindle Edition).
[13] Peterson, Jordan, *Maps of Meaning* (New York: Routledge, 1999)., p. 3.
[14] Ibid., p. 4.

the singularity of Will to Power by downplaying the very belief in any substantial grounding beyond the aesthetic. Finally, Peterson took for granted that any object of experience can be construed either as a mythological significance or as a scientific essence. The author of the present text, however, would suggest that a simple binary of layers fails to capture a complexity which Kant himself recognized by positing a journey from raw sense data to rationally-intelligible experience that incorporated more than just the two layers of "sense contents in" and "temporally-unified, rationally-intelligible experience out." The present text will require a similarly "transcendental" turn.

In other words, the author disagrees with Greer that a simple dualism between mythology of progress and underlying fossil fuel resource base is sufficient to capture the complexity of a hierarchy of levels that employs a number of intermediary structures of meaning in between material petroleum and its manifestation in a mythology of progress. The five layers the author will propose do not denote five different objects any more than Jordan Peterson's dualism between a mode of significance and a mode of essence denote two different objects: in both cases, there is only one substance which can be "construed" either mythically or scientifically. Petroleum occupies the deepest position within the author's own hierarchy of layers of meaningfulness (the Somatic layer, as will be explicated in greater detail) but it is not at all absent from the higher layers of Memology, Sense Objectivity, System, and Mythology. Oil's presence in these higher layers is, in fact, the basis for the truth of any of these seemingly unrelated spheres of meaning. The substance of Oil is not somewhere beyond the appearance as situated in Mythology or any of the other higher order layers of meaning: the substance of Oil is rather always already *in* the appearance, since Fossil Fuels make up the very substance of consciousness in our era.

*The Five Transcendental Registers of Meaning*

The present discussion will conclude with a table that will demonstrate this admittedly-obscure claim. First, however, a brief description of each layer will be necessary. In each of the following five layers, the same substance is manifested differently according to the unique requirements of each frame of givenness, insofar as each layer is a distinct transcendental register bound by its own structural features which provide unique criteria for generating meaning. In the deepest Somatic Layer (from the Ancient Greek term "σῶμα" for a physical body with a real existence), petroleum is given to consciousness merely as a presence. Although it may sound indefensible to argue that presence can be meaningful even in the absence of imagistic coherence as a definite object, a modern citizen of Fossil Fuel Modernity could conceivable pass his or her entire life without ever seeing a physical barrel of petroleum but that person would still live with a vague intuition of the massively-powerful presence of petroleum. In fact, presence could arguably be considered to be Kant's Thing in Itself's only non-negative predicate: the only thing one can positively about it is that it is present, for if it were not, the entire set of appearances which indirectly triangulate it would certainly vanish into nothingness.[15]

In his book *Jesus Before the Gospels: How the Earliest Christians Remembered, Invented, and Changed Stories of the Saviour*, New Testament scholar Bart Ehrman argued that stories of Jesus' appearing to his disciples after his death likely provided the impetus for the Christian religion to develop even after its central figure was known by everyone to have been put to death.[16] Ehrman did not explicitly pass judgment on the truth value of any of these visions of Jesus, which even Paul, someone who had never met Jesus during his lifetime, claimed to have had. Ehrman instead emphasized that in any case one must adopt the psychological concept of "veridicity" (from the Latin word "veritas" for truth) to distinguish experiences in which the intended object really exists from fantasies, hallucinations, and dreams, in which it does not. An intuition in which the intended object really existed would be veridic; an intuition in which it did not exist would be non-veridic.

---

[15] Kant, Immanuel, *The Critique of Pure Reason* (London: Penguin, 2007), p. 65.
[16] Ehrman, Bart, *Jesus Before the Gospels: How the Earliest Christians Remembered, Invented, and Changed Stories of the Saviour* (New York: HarperCollins, 2016).

It is interesting to note that although even Jordan Peterson characterized Phenomenology as an ideal science of the abstract structures of experience which remain after dropping the real object of experience from consideration, Edmund Husserl actually entertained similar concerns regarding the veridicty of experience by arguing that "illusion" and "hallucination" were not "genuine" experiences.[17] In a genuine experience, one could "confirm" the "presence" of the object in the "actual context of experience" in order to establish that "the perceived thing is real and itself really given, and that [it is] bodily [present] in perception."[18] It is interesting that Husserl also chose to designate "bodily presence" (if he had used transliterated Greek, "somatic parousia") as the criteria of veridicity.

The author of the present volume will also adopt the term "veridic" to distinguish the truth-modes by which somatic givenness might establish itself according to the criteria of this deepest level of the transcendental hierarchy of meanings. Contrary to expectation, determining whether one's consciousness of the Soma is veridic (true) or not requires no visual counterpart. Part II of the present work shall explain that somatic presence is irreducible to visual image or any other determinate sense content because somatic presence is the very foundation which allows a world to be disclosed in which such perceptions would be accessible in the first place. The Soma's absence will similarly lack any visual requirements. After Petroleum's disappearance, one will not have to explicitly register that no empirical barrels of petroleum occupy one's line of sight to recognize that a seismic shift had occurred which will shake the very foundations of one's worldview. Petroleum's disappearance will likewise be experienced in the near future either as a raw absence that is properly recognized as such or as a ghost essence which the delusional misread as a continued presence, to their own detriment.

The second layer, the Memological, presents the same fossil fuel substance through the transcendental criteria of a shape: in this case, living under Fossil Fuel Modernity means having a

---

[17] Husserl, Edmund, *Ideas* (Eastford: Martino Fine Books, 2017), p. 127.
[18] Ibid. P. 127.

geometrical bias below the surface which distorts one's expectations by coercing one's interpretation of higher-order contents to fit a shape of progress. This progress is expressed geometrically as the "deep meme" of an ascending arrow which never retracts and never plateaus. Mythologies, objects, and systems understood from the higher levels therefore can only be understood if they hold a minimal isomorphic fit with this underlying shape of progress which is itself merely the substance of fossil fuels given to intuition as a memological shape rather than as a somatic presence.

Of course, societies not dominated by the burning of fossil fuels will lack the deep meme of linear ascending progress because the geometrical bias embodied in a ray that never retracts and never plateaus is just a way to present the somatic presence of petroleum, coal, and natural gas within the transcendental requirements of a shape rather than as a raw presence. In contrast with the shape of linear progress, the Hunter Gatherer worldview embodies the deep meme of a level plane in which humans naturalize culture by interpreting their own contingent beliefs and customs as an extension of the reified and eternal order of Nature, while they anthropomorphise Nature by interpreting flora, fauna, astrological bodies, and meteorological phenomena as pseudo-social entities capable of being influenced through ritual. This Hunter Gatherer deep meme is itself just the natural resource base of wild game, wild roots, and other foraging materials viewed through the unique transcendental structures of Memology.

In addition, the Agrarian Worldview embodies the geometrical bias of a circle, in which completeness rather than infinite growth is the implicit definition of perfection and repeating cycles rather than open-ended progress are the implicit temporal schema by which to interpret historical and personal events. This abstract shape of a circle is itself just the agricultural resource base of cyclically-planted grain mapped onto the transcendental structure of Memology rather than the somatic structure of presence.

Finally, John Michael Greer has suggested that the era of Fossil Fuels will be followed by an era of salvage in which the massive infrastructure built to suit the needs of industrialism will linger as a set of ruins that will have to be repurposed for new tasks unimagined by the engineers who only envisioned them serving the needs of a culture awash in cheap, easily-accessible, abundant fossil fuels.[19] The author proposes that this era will have its own deep meme by which to reinterpret the "same" objects through a radically different geometrical bias: the deep meme of Salvage will present the lingering memory of a past age of abundance but will posit the era of Fossil Fuels as an historical anomaly never to be repeated. It is not coincidental that the bell curve is the geometrical shape that isomorphically captures the Mathematics of Hubbert's original Peak Oil models. The deep meme of the bell curve is already literally memologically isomorphic to the reality of fossil fuel depletion, even before it has colonized an historical era's consciousness. Likewise, the bell curve's main value stems from its being the only one of the four deep memes that can explicitly posit "decline" as a memological schema by which to structure a world. The following table synopsizes each of the four deep memes:

[1]

| Worldview | Deep Meme | Soma | Transcendental Shape |
|---|---|---|---|
| Hunter Gatherer | Level Plane | Woolly Mammoth, Deer, Wild Roots | ▬ |
| Agrarian | Circle | Grain, Cattle, Sheep | ● |
| Fossil Fuel | Infinite Ray | Petroleum, Natural Gas, Coal | ● (with ray) |

---

[19] Greer, John Michael, "The Age of Salvage," in *The Archdruid Report* Vol 1. (Chicago: Founders House, 2017), p. 304.

| Salvage | Bell Curve | Industrial-Era Salvage Materials | (bell curve) |

  Higher than the layer of Memology, the Sense Objective layer presents the same fossil fuel substance in the form of a definite object which "makes sense" to intuition on the basis of its ability to manifest the worldview of Fossil Fuel Modernity even in the absence of words. A machine, for example, is an object which be utterly unintelligible to a prehistoric hunter gatherer or to a medieval agrarian peasant because the Fossil Fuel Worldview is not only a subjective requirement to grasp it; it is also the very content of the object itself. A machine embodies the fossil fuel worldview by promising that burning the remaining reserves of fossil fuels out of existence will somehow be sufficient to solve every problem afflicting humankind: even, paradoxically, the problems *caused by* using machines, such as Climate Change, resource depletion, and mass unemployment from automation.

  One historical anomaly is that in Hunter Gatherer and Agrarian contexts this layer is populated by sense objects: only in Fossil Fuel Modernity is it primarily filled with "counter sense objects" which embody a worldview which is inherently illogical. The following examples of sense and counter sense objects demonstrate this distinction. A well, for example, is a sense object: from the well, a clearly finite supply of water must be drawn by hand through lowering a bucket which, in turn, can only hold a finite amount of water, not even a drop of which can be wasted. The agrarian deep meme of finite resources, manual labour to accomplish tasks, and yearly cycles by which the monsoon rains must replenish what had been depleted during the dry season in India are all embodied in the modest image of a pail of well water. The faucet in a kitchen sink in a modern suburban home in North America, however, is a counter sense object; even though the supply of water is finite (and, if the house is located in a south-western desert city like Phoenix or Las Vegas, it is frighteningly finite) the user has no sense of this finitude and merely registers the tap as a device from which an infinite amount of water might be drawn at no cost to the user or ecosystem beyond the water bill paid each month. The counter sense object only makes sense because it reiterates the deep meme of fossil fuels, in which an infinite return is promised to emerge from an origin which is either ambiguous or blatantly posited as arising out of thin air.

Similarly, a compost pit is a sense object. Food scraps from the kitchen are not really a waste product so much as they are raw materials which can be converted back into an immensely-useful resource if combined with the modest inputs of leaves, ashes, moisture, and a small amount of manual labour each day. Some months later, rich black compost will provide nutrition to the next generation of vegetables in the garden which, in turn, will eventually find their way back into the compost pit. A compost pit is not an anonymous blob of colours and smells which must be subsumed under some systematic linguistic label or even some mythological personality in order to make sense. Overlapping with a deep meme already available to the subject on the basis of the Soma's presence is sufficient for the sense object to make sense to the subject.

A plastic trash can in a North American suburban garage is, on the other hand, a counter sense object. Rather than invest a minute amount of labour into salvaging valuable nutrients left behind in the potato peelings, fruit peels, and coffee grounds left behind after each day of living, the clueless suburbanite will throw these nutrient-rich contents into a garbage bag, indiscriminately mixing them with toxic chemicals and plastic trash in the process. Once per week, a noisy truck will pull up to the house to carry these "away" and the suburbanite will pat himself or herself on the back for being responsible enough to "do his or her part." What that person will not realize is that there is no such place as away, and that each load of garbage he or she sends to the landfill will only feed the exploding rat population and damage the environment.[20]

---

[20] The author acknowledges his own indebtedness to John Michael Greer for writing on a similar topic in a late 2007 post of the *Archdruid Report*.
Greer, John Michael, "Agriculture: Closing the Circle" in *The Archdruid Report*, Vol 1 (Chicago: Founders House, 2017), p. 348.

The absurdity of believing that trash "goes away" just because you throw it into a plastic can and then wait for a garbage truck to arrive once per week is the kind of counter sense which passes as rational sense only because the trash can is a counter sense object that isomorphically overlaps with the deep meme of fossil fuels and the Soma of Petroleum.

Above the Sense Objective Layer, the Systematic Layer, which might also be called the Gnostic Layer for its emphasis on systematic knowledge ("γνῶσῖς"), differs by generating sprawling systems which paradoxically get larger and larger without ever stating as clearly in thousands or even millions of symbols what can be expressed quite clearly and coherently in the single object of a sense object or the single shape of a deep meme. Despite the façade of scientific objectivity, systems are never just eternally-valid sets of truths free from bias, yet the bias hard-wired into systems cannot be reduced subjective prejudice: systems reduplicate the biases of the sense objects, deep memes, and somatic substances which underlie them because a system is, quite literally, just another manifestation of the same somatic resource base within the requirements imposed by a systematic disclosure of meaning rather than a memological, sense objective, or somatic one. For example, the modern "science" of Artificial "Intelligence" so fanatically-celebrated by the media is just a sprawling redundancy of the counter sense object of a machine, the deep meme of progress, and the somatic base of fossil fuel energy. The Google Algorithm, for example, states less clearly in two billion lines what could be expressed perfectly clearly in just the raw presencing power of the somatic resource base. This is because the minimal unit of gnostic meaning is an abstract value systematically related to an uncountably-vast number of other abstract values, whereas the soma can merely presence itself independently of any other factor to communicate the same substance much more powerfully.

Finally, Mythology expresses the same fossil fuel resource base but is beholden to a transcendental structure of disclosure distinct from systematic value, sense objective form, memological shape, or somatic presence. The minimal unit of meaning for Mythology is not, as one might naively think, a character, a prop, or even a central conflict. The minimal unit is an event which is disclosed as a primordial unity which can only later be segmented down into smaller pieces like a set of characters. An example from Hindu Mythology will illustrate this: when Lord Brahma created the beautiful maiden Shatarupa and fell in love with his own creation, she fled from his line of sight; he responded, as the god of creation, by just generating another head whose line of sight encompassed the area to which she had fled. She responded, predictably, by moving again but he repeated this gesture until he had four heads that encompassed the full horizontal circumference outside his body. When she fled upwards to avoid the line of sight of all four heads, he generated another on top of his head, but just then Shiva, god of destruction, sliced off this fifth head, imposing both a physical limit on his gaze and a religious limit on where he could be worshipped.[21]

Although one certainly *could* break up the event of "Lord Shiva cutting off Brahma's fifth head to protect Shatarupa and limit where he could be worshipped" into a set of smaller pieces, such as "Lord Shiva," "Lord Brahma," "Shatarupa," "the sword," and "the severed fifth head," this would be as contrived and secondary as breaking up a word into smaller morphemes, such as deriving "un," "cann", and "y" from the word "uncanny." Human dwelling is primarily mythological and similarly unfolds according to the smooth logic of disclosing coherent events which can only be decomposed into smaller pieces through some act of abstraction.

One can only deviate into systematic, sense objective, memological, and somatic frames of intuition through a conscious act which suspends the mythological horizon which would otherwise remain undisturbed. The primary challenge of Peak Oil Philosophy is that the Mythology of Progress is disclosed so unproblematically to virtually all citizens of Fossil Fuel Modernity that the other layers (above all, the Soma) are effectively invisible to them. The purpose of this book will largely be to wilfully disrupt that smooth flow of mythological meaningfulness in order to alert the reader to the complicated series of mediations which reveal that

---

[21]Murty, Sudha, "Brahma's Folly" in *The Man from the Egg* (Haryana: Puffin, 2017).

unquestioned mythological significance to be nothing more than a euphemism for the immense amounts of fossil fuels required to sustain it. It would be impossible to make any sense of the Mythology of the American Dream without sublime amounts of fossil fuels: behind the comforting images of a white picket fence suburban middle class lifestyle lies the ideology that it is desirable to spend one's entire life sitting in air-conditioned buildings or driving over hundreds of miles of suburban wasteland each week while outsourcing the nation's agricultural production from skilled farmers to tractors and pesticide-spraying airplanes, outsourcing the manufacturing sector from blacksmiths to overseas factory machines, and even outsourcing thinking itself from human minds to energy-hungry armies of artificially "intelligent" machines. A conscious leap from the mythological to the somatic layer reveals that this entire venture amounts to giving up more and more human abilities on the gamble that there will always be enough fossil fuels left over to power the billions of machines sprawled over the face of the Earth, let alone to counter the adverse effects of environmental destruction, toxic pollution, mass extinction, and carcinogenic exposure which are the unstated results of the same "technological progress." The following table summarizes the preceding discussion:
[2]

| Layer of Meaning | Example | Minimal Unit of Meaning |
|---|---|---|
| Somatic | Fossil Fuels | Presence |
| Memological | Ascending Arrow of Progress | Shape |
| Sense Objective | Machine | Form |
| Systematic | Artificial Intelligence | Value |
| Mythological | Myth of the American Dream | Event |

## *The Return of Substance: The History of Western Philosophy in Retrospect*

It is not that each layer presents a different object, such that one would be confronted with the preposterous notion of five different worlds through which the subject might transition by adopting a different standpoint for each one, a "quintuplist" stance far more unacceptable to Modern Rationalism than any dualism of merely two layers. Rather, the paradox is how even though there is only one world, there is no neutral frame through which it might be disclosed exactly as it is, a fact which Kant sought to express through the notion of a Thing in Itself which is inaccessible to intuition because if one has achieved givenness in intuition, one has already been restricted by the immanent requirements to which intuition is beholden in order to be given subjectively.[22] Kant realized that these requirements of intuition are not intrinsic properties of the Thing in Itself but structural features unique to a particular frame of intuition; for example, if one has achieved an intuition of the world, one will have already distorted the Thing in Itself's true nature by having to present it within spatial and temporal coordinates which are indigenous to the transcendental subject itself rather than to the Thing.

Although the author agrees with Kant's basic insight that one cannot gain intuition of the world without being beholden first to the a priori structures by which any intuition must be given, one could argue that Kant's main error lay in incorporating several intermediary stages in the background of what was still, at the end, just one single "finished product" of smooth-flowing, rationally-intelligible, temporally-unified experience. That is to say, Kant posited the stages of synthetic constitution to occur deep within the darkness of subjective interiority, such that one could only indirectly reconstruct an idea of the phases by working backwards from the "finished product" of the appearance. Kant's stages (such as sense data impinging on the senses, which is then organized into space and time, and later subsumed under the notion) do not

---

[22] Kant, Immanuel, *The Critique of Pure Reason* (London: Penguin, 2007), p. 67.

actually occur as determinate phases which the subject can directly see.

The author of the present volume will differ from Kant by suggesting that the five layers of meaning are not procedural stages of a single algorithm which could only be indirectly reconstructed through a forensic analysis of the content of finished intuition; instead, each layer really *can* be considered in isolation because each holds an equally legitimate claim to Phenomenological disclosure. The Mythic register of meaning, bound by the immanent criteria of the event, is the default stance by which human dwelling on the earth ordinarily occurs; in Heideggerian language, one does not need to explicitly enter into the Mythic horizon, since one will find that one was already dwelling there. Still, transitioning to the Gnostic Layer of Systematic Meaning is a routine activity which can be accomplished simply by adopting a different transcendental framework of intuition that privileges the disclosure of value determined by an implicit system of rank rather than the disclosure of a mythic event populated by characters struggling against an implicit central conflict. Deviating further into the realm of Sense Objectivity similarly can be accomplished through adopting a different transcendental frame in which the minimal unit of meaning is no longer systematic value defined through rank or mythic event defined through conflict but rather objective form defined by its embodiment of a worldview in a coherent object that makes sense to intuition even in the absence of words (such as a machine's ability to embody the Modern Fossil Fuel Worldview while being utterly incomprehensible to a prehistoric hunter gatherer.) Deep Memes similarly present meaning with a different transcendental structure of intelligibility by redefining meaning as abstract geometrical shape. Even in the absence of any particular content, the geometrical bias of an ascending ray that never retracts and never plateaus can embody the same Fossil Fuel Worldview memologically. Finally, the most unnatural stance which requires the furthest deviation from the natural mythical stance of dwelling (yet for precisely that reason, the most foundational of all the layers), is the Somatic Layer in which raw presence and absence that denote the existence or non-existence of a particular physical body are sufficient to denote meaning according to the structural requirements of somatic veridicity. It is not that somatic presence is merely an imperfect version of memological shape, sense objective form, systematic value, or mythic event; each is a distinct and unique register of meaning which cannot be reduced to the others without resulting in catastrophic misunderstandings.

### *Philosophical Confusion is Transcendental Bias*

Many of the errors of Philosophy have stemmed from fixating on one transcendental register of meaning and either ignoring the other four (that is, denying their existence) or coercing them to fit the criteria of this one preferred register. Marxists prided themselves to be "radical materialists" yet the Marxist analysis fails to penetrate below the layer of sense objectivity, let alone all the way down to the bottom of the hierarchy to which they remain blind precisely by remaining too rigidly fixed to an interpretation that equates "matter" with "object." The Marxist notion of modes of production is simply a fixation on the layer of sense objects. Marx believed that changes in relations of production followed from technological advances. The Spinning Jenny, for example, was the technological change which the bourgeoisie profited from in order to displace the landed aristocracy who remained stuck at the level of manual labour and hand tools (wielded by armies of serfs rather than the aristocracy themselves, of course.) A modern factory employing sophisticated computerized machines has made even the Spinning Jenny seem quite primitive, and the technological aristocracy who have become enormously wealthy from this change would cause the fortunes of the early industrial bourgeoisie to seem quaint in comparison. Marx's vision for Communist Progress is largely just the belief that another technological change will usher in an era in which the machines of the Communist Era will be so much more sophisticated that they will displace the capitalist factory owners through ushering in a set of machines that make the capitalists' seem primitive in comparison.

Marx's failure to provide a useful response to industrialist inequality stemmed from the fact that although he claimed to penetrate all the way to the "material conditions" of Industrialism, he merely isolated the sense objective layer of technological innovation. Modern Technology is, however, far from the deepest layer open to analysis, as it is merely a sense objective euphemism for an energy resource whose intrinsic nature as somatic substance is irreducible to any sense object's ability to indirectly manifest it. Marx's emphasis on the "modes of production uncritically takes for granted that Communism will occur under the deep meme of progress and the somatic presence of coal, in that Communism is every bit as dependent upon burning fossil fuels to accomplish "progress" as Capitalism is. The ecological disasters that occurred in the Soviet Union were predictable to anyone who was not too blinded by the deep meme of progress and the Soma of Fossil Fuels to see just how risky it is to gamble on trying out new half-understood approaches to agriculture and energy production that rely on toxic chemicals and energy-intensive machines.

Marxism is therefore just the mistaken belief that isolating the transcendental layer of sense objectivity can serve as a universal skeleton key to unlock all of the other four layers of meaning, if one does not just deny their existence altogether. Marx's view that ideology is just the reiteration of modes of production should not be misread as an insight into the author's own hierarchy of five layers of meaning: what Marx really suggested was that Mythology and Gnostic Systems are both just the Sense Object of machines (or in archaic examples, the Sense Object of pre-modern tools) in disguise.

The Unabomber Ted Kaczynski also overemphasized the sense objective layer but still acknowledged that systems and mythology are distinct registers rather than ideological distortions of the "one true layer." In one sense, he was correct to argue that it will be useless to address the mythology or even the systems of modernity without penetrating to the deeper layer of sense objectivity (what he normally just calls "Technology") upon which they are founded. Much of his argument in his last published work *Anti-Tech Revolution* revolved around his insistence that the revolutionary movement must have *only one* "single, clear, and concrete objective" and that objective must be the destruction of technology.[23] Even issues as empirically-urgent as environmental destruction must not be allowed to supersede technology and become an end in themselves. He warns that if the revolutionary movement engages with those concerned about environmental damage specifically, they must "make very clear that the environmental issue is a sideshow and that the long-term goal must be to eliminate the entire technological system." This is not due to a disregard for the extreme seriousness of the problem of ecological destruction, since Kaczynski holds a far more apocalyptic view of the Earth's long-term inhabitability than any of the Democrat Party congressmen and women who are "deeply concerned about Climate Change" but apparently not deeply concerned enough to cut down the number of casual flights from their home district in California to their second residency in Washington, D. C., let alone to stop driving a car or to consider the carbon footprint of providing air conditioning to a mansion in Florida year-round.

On the contrary, Kaczynski warns that even the basic Ancient Greek elements cannot be taken for granted into the far future: earth, wind, fire, and air seemed in the Ancient World to be indestructible givens, basic bodies impossible to decompose to simpler elements.[24] But in the far future we will not be able to take for granted something as basic as whether there will be air to breathe:

> Most people take our atmosphere for granted, as though Providence had decreed once and for all that air should consist of 78% Nitrogen, 21% oxygen, and 1% other gases. In reality, our atmosphere in its present form was created, and is still maintained by living things [most of which are in danger of eventual extinction][25]

---

[23] Kaczynski, Ted, *Anti-Tech Revolution: Why and How* (Scottsdale: Fitch & Madison, 2015), p. 90 and p. 154.
[24] In his lexicon of terms in Book V of *The Metaphysics*, Aristotle designates earth, fire, and water to be examples of "simple bodies" which provide the basic building blocks for the more complicated bodies such as "animals." Aristotle, *The Metaphysics*, in *Basic Works of Aristotle* (New York: The Modern Library, 2002), p. 761.

Water is another basic element the existence of which cannot be taken for granted into the far future. In fact, the Earth of the far future may come to resemble the planet Venus:

> Addition of gasses capable of trapping heat could accelerate the release of $H_2O$ and raise the temperature to a point where the oceans would evaporate . . . Some believe that such changes may have occurred on Venus[26]

The paradox Kaczynski correctly noticed was that one will not be able to save even something as vitally important as water or air by simply radicalizing one's concern for water and air. Their disappearance would not occur in an idealistic vacuum in which the only meaningful standard would be how explicitly one was concerned about saving them. In fact, devoting all of one's time to this issue will only waste energy that would be better redirected to focusing on the one issue that actually could make a difference: Modern Technology. Environmentalist worry will be useless to accomplish anything unless it is paired with a recognition that the broader systems destroying the very possibility of life on Earth are all just reiterations of the same single, remarkably coherent sense object of the machine.

There is no question for Ted Kaczynski that the machine must be physically destroyed. Anyone in the movement who plays games with trying to reform technology to remove its negative effects will only guarantee that the movement itself will be sterilized into uselessness. His repeated warnings that the movement must be strictly opposed to Leftism stems from his realization that the sublime power of Technology will simply be far too great a temptation for the Leftists to resist if offered control over it.[27] We need not wait for some hypothetical future to display this

---

[25] Kaczynski, Ted, *Anti-Tech Revolution: Why and How* (Scottsdale: Fitch & Madison, 2015), p. 64.
[26] Ibid., p.67.
[27] Kaczynski, Ted, *Industrial Society and its Future*, in *Technological Slavery* (Port Townsend: Feral House, 2010), p. 106.

paradox, as even today it is not a coincidence that the most liberal metropolitan areas of the United States, such as Seattle and the San Francisco Bay Area, congratulate themselves on banning plastic straws from coffee shops but fight for even *more growth* in the technological industries that are driving the very same pollution and Climate Change sweeping the globe; they are creating a gigantic, sprawling monster into which one single politically-correct gesture put on display for the news cameras will fail to make any significant dent. Likewise, Kaczynski implies that trusting leftists to get rid of Modern Technology is about as recklessly foolish as trusting any other power-hungry figure with Frodo's ring. Gandfal's warning in the first volume of *The Lord of the Rings* can just as easily be applied to the gamble that leftists could be trusted to destroy Modern Technology after assuming control of the nation, control which would be impossible to maintain *without* the use of machines:

> We cannot use the Ruling Ring. It is altogether evil. Its strength is too great for anyone to wield at will, save those who have already a great power of their own. But for them it holds an even deadlier peril. The very desire of it corrupts the heart.'[28]

Although the author agrees fully with Kaczynski's warning, the author objects to Kaczynski's view that Technology is the ultimate foundation to be removed if the vicious self-propagating systems built on top of it are to be stopped from destroying the (habitable) Earth in the quest for their own power.[29] Technology (or more precisely, the counter sense object of a machine) is similarly dependent upon some lower foundation, without which it would rendered just as illusory and impotent as the systems and

---

[28] Tolkien, J. R. R., *The Lord of the Rings* (London: HarperCollins, 2005), p.267.
[29] The second chapter of Kaczynski's *Anti-Tech Revolution* is devoted to establishing the laws of behaviour for self-propagating systems. This behaviour is already destructive enough but reaches apocalyptic levels when combined with Modern Technology. Kaczsynki, Ted, *Anti-Tech Revolution* (Scottsdale: Fitch and Madison, 2015), p. 42.

mythologies based upon it. Kaczynski's Technology would not just lose a part of its intelligibility if it were deprived of the underlying deep meme of Progress or if it were deprived of the underlying Soma of Fossil Fuels: it would cease to exist altogether. In a far future world completely devoid of fossil fuels, a machine would not be a machine: its very essence would be transformed from the entity powerful enough to literally destroy the elements of air and water into a useless, ugly heap of rusting garbage on the side of some rustic dirt road where shepherds lead their flocks on the path to greener pastures and donkey carts carry loads of pottery to the market to be bartered in exchange for vegetables or milk. Even the physical body of a machine is not the ultimate independent entity which discloses the deeply problematic world in which we live today; it is itself just a dependent entity which only has any being insofar as it borrows its share of being from some more solid foundation. That foundation is Fossil Fuels.

Mistaking a sense object for a universal key to understand all other phenomena is not the only error which philosophers have made regarding the five registers of meaning. Analytic Philosophy can largely be considered to be a reduction of the five registers of meaning to the one layer of the Systematic-Gnostic Meaning, either in the form of Logic (Russell, Frege) or Language Games (Wittgenstein). The Continental Philosophy proponents of the Linguistic Turn may be surprised to find that they have committed the same error by reinterpreting all five layers of meaning to be the gnostic layer in disguise, by arguing that "everything is language." The author recognises that Analytic and Linguistic Turn philosophers have made many important contributions toward understanding the gnostic layer of systematic meaning. Yet the author could hardly imagine a more dangerous act than reinterpreting Peak Oil as a merely linguistic or systematic problem born from an empty language game. Explicitly recognizing that the dimension of Somatic Existence has nothing intrinsically to do with Linguistics, Logic, or any other system will be the only viable path towards doing justice to life or death seriousness of Peak Oil.

*Usury at the Gates*

To consider another important example of how the five layers of meaning overlap, it is remarkable that usury could have progressed from its former position as the ultimate economic scandal to a commonplace fact taken for granted as necessary to live a "normal life," though this has largely devolved into a euphemism for circulating through each month's mortgage, student loan, car payment, and medical debt bills in a cycle of indebtedness from which one can never escape. Dante's decision to locate usurers lower in hell than murderers did not stem from some archaic ignorance about "the benefits of Modern Finance." It stemmed from a medieval wisdom about how pre-fossil fuel economies work which we have forgotten at our own peril as the temporary economic surpluses from fossil fuels misled us to think that the expectation that there will "always be more growth later to cover the interest on a huge debt" was a reasonable bet upon which to hinge an entire lifetime of payment obligations. Yet Dante did not just condemn usury as sinful on pious religious grounds which could be rejected out of hand as irrelevant to non-Medieval Catholic contexts. He argued that usury was a vicious attack against the order of *Nature* herself:

> From art and nature, if you will recall
> The opening of Genesis, man is meant
> To earn his way and further humankind.
> But still the usurer takes another way;
> He scorns nature and her follower, art,
> Because he puts his hope in something else[30]

Aristotle shared Dante's belief that usury was a radical deviation away from the order of Nature by warning that financial intermediation intrinsically opens the pathway for economic perversion by introducing a disconnect between the set of tangible goods, the value which is determined by objective form, which make up an intrinsically finite set; and the set of financial

---

[30] Dante, *The Inferno*, Canto XI, l.106-112

abstractions, a set which can theoretically be expanded to infinity. Usury, even by the standard of financial manipulation in general, ranked as the absolute "worst" because it abandoned any connection to form whatsoever in favour of this perverse illusion of generating wealth from wealth:

> The most hated sort [of economic perversions], and with the greatest reason, is usury, which makes a gain out of money itself and not from the natural object of it[31]

Even Martin Luther displayed an abhorrence for usury by referring to the usurer as a code word for the "worst of all possible sinners" in his *Treatise on Good Works*. Luther argued that going through the motions of performing pious rituals in the guise of doing "good works" to earn one's salvation could never save even the least sinful of all sinners, because the empty symbolic rituals of Roman Catholicism were so empty and so limited to exterior appearance that they could be performed perfectly well even by the very worst of all sinners, the usurers:

> For nowadays they say that the [good] works ... are singing, reading, organ playing, reading the mass, saying the matins and vespers and the other hours, the founding and decorating of churches, altars, and monastic houses ... although these things [even] the usurers, adulterers and all manner of sinners can do too, and do them daily.[32]

Unfortunately, Aristotle's, Dante's, and Martin Luther's wisdom on the topic have devolved from eternally useful advice to some fossilized relic of history which, it is claimed, only evidences how poorly Ancient and Medieval Man understood the "rigorous science of Economics." In fact, today acceptance of usury has become so commonplace that the same devout Roman Catholic and

---

[31] Aristotle, *The Politics*, in *Basic Works of Aristotle* (New York: Modern Library, 2001), p. 1141.
[32] Luther, Martin, *A Treatise on Good Works*, Kindle Edition.

Protestant Christian churchgoers whose ancestors would have abhorred usury as among the most evil of all sins now find no ethical contradiction between their religious beliefs and their career earning a comfortable salary working in the financial industry. The irony that much of the modern churches' financial balance sheet is indirectly gained from the practice of usury can be left to the reader to contemplate.

Despite the fact that usury has become so commonplace now that one could easily imagine a devout Christian young man or woman praying very hard to get a high-paying position as a professional usurer a financial institution without seeing the blatant religious contradiction in such an act, it would be deeply intellectually dishonest to downplay the deadly seriousness which past attitudes demonstrated towards usury. The medieval penalty of capital punishment for usurers may seem barbaric to modern politically correct sensibilities but it will likely (and, quite arguably, *justifiably*) make a comeback in future times when such attitudes about usury's utterly-destructive effect on economies (especially economies that cannot bet on cheating their way to unearned growth by stealing energy from fossil fuels) again become the economic norm. It would be difficult to imagine that public hangings could *not* again become popular ways to "deal with usurers" in the far post-oil future of, say, 2195. It is also likely that the religious institutions will change their minds once again on usury and restore its place within the list of worst sins.

The idea that paying back interest on a debt that was far too large for the borrower to handle from the start will *not* lead to economic devastation for the borrower and unearned prosperity for the parasitic lender can only be justified if one presumes that fossil fuels will provide more growth later to cover the interest which is unaffordable now.

This is because a loan (and particularly a student loan) is just the counter sense object of a bottomless pit. Even if one throws all of his or her money down the rat-hole of trying to pay off a student loan, one will find that the loan has grown even larger and that one has been put into default, in which case the company will be given the right to take even more away from someone who has already given them everything. This is not merely an individual problem of "irresponsible borrowers": Richard Heinberg has documented the shocking fact that because "economic growth" under Fossil Fuels required constant exponential increases in debt, there is currently more debt issued than there is total money; even if you collected every dollar (all of which were printed at will anyway) into a bag and tried to pay the debts, there would still be an outstanding debt that had to somehow to be paid back with money that doesn't exist.[33] We are literally being asked to do the impossible and then being punished personally when we cannot. The notion of Student Loan "Forgiveness" is intentionally misleading since even those desperate enough to seek it are forced to tacitly admit that they were the ones who did something wrong, whereas they were just the victims of a colossal Ponzi Scheme that has engulfed the entire world.[34] To say that a bottomless pit for which the amount of money owed is more than the total amount of money that exists makes no sense logically is to understate the problem considerably, yet it is also to admit that its acceptance is simply due to its overlap with the Soma of Fossil Fuels and the deep meme of linear ascent.

In other words, our modern acceptance of usury simply is a half-understood glimpse into the reality of living under fossil fuels. Of course, one could argue that even in an era dominated by fossil fuels, like our own, this attitude that debt is harmless or even beneficial is still completely false. Alan Collinge's independent work as the sole honest voice about the Student Loan Usury Catastrophe has revealed that the only escape from six figure student loan debts which routinely double, triple, and quadruple in size for no reason except sheer greed lie in the bleak options of suicide, assuming a fake identity, or fleeing the country.[35] The

---

[33] Heinberg, Richard, *The End of Growth: Adapting to Our New Economic Reality* (Gabriola Island: New Society Publishers, 2011), p. 72.
[34] Thank you to flowersarelovesome for this comment.
[35] The references to suicide in Collinge's book are not hyperbole. In addition to several confirmed suicides that resulted from student loans (pp. 63-4), Collinge documents the stories of borrowers who only narrowly escaped suicide through fleeing the country to relocate in Asia. Of course, the author does not think this

author himself writes from the position of a student loan refugee who fled across the Modern Imperial Frontiers into the so-called "Third World" in order to escape the same excessive financial burdens which led many Romans to make a similar escape into the "barbarian lands" in the final years of that empire's decline.

Agrarian contexts *a priori* rule out giant surpluses as anything except either unique, unrepeatable historical anomalies or the stuff of fantasy, projected back into a distant "Golden Age" or projected forward into a coming utopia. The author's mother has anecdotally recounted living as a South Korean peasant in a mud home in the rural mountains after the Korean War, at a time when infrastructural destruction from the war was so severe that even eating rice rather than barley was considered a great luxury. A childhood of working barefoot in the rice paddies in order to not face the bleak alternative of starvation led to memories of leeches on her legs which recurred in bad dreams for many years later. Pigs and cows lingered on site, providing valuable meat but occasionally containing dangerous worms which would end up in the peasants' biological systems. These are but a few of the real life summaries of living an agrarian existence which will likely sound like legends even to a modern South Korean, but this modern highly-technologized Korea differs from the village of the author's mother's childhood only by adding one element: fossil fuels.

At any rate, agrarian contexts which lack fossil fuels simply rule out the possibility of paying back interest on a loan with "more growth later on" because it would unspeakably irresponsible to assume that "more growth later on" is guaranteed to happen and, even more so, to assume that you will personally benefit from it even if it does. The wisdom of living in a context in which surpluses either don't happen at all, or only happen temporarily, can be summarized in the Biblical account of seven years of surplus followed by seven years of famine. Such a story would be literally unthinkable to a modern thinker for whom "surplus" has simply

---

a useful solution to the problem but this uncomfortable fact must be brought out of the silence into which the shameless, morally-bankrupt media has forced it. Collinge, Alan, *The Student Loan Scam: The Most Oppressive Debt in U.S. History and How We Can Fight Back* (Boston: Beacon Press, 2009), pp. 58-62.

become the default expectation. One need not even explicitly posit surplus as an object that must be laboriously constructed as such; surplus already pervades our entire worldview, even to the extent that it has become so "present" to intuition that one can no longer even recognize it as such. Surplus is not an object that occurs for seven years and then disappears. Surplus simply is the shape which consciousness in fossil fuel modernity holds, such that one *always* sees surplus because "seeing surpluses" is as redundant transcendentally as "seeing with eyes" is biologically. This transcendental presupposition is the *only* thing that lead us all to accept a crime so reprehensible, risky, and illogical as universally handing out six figure student loan debts to kids not even old enough to vote and who will live through the era of fossil fuel depletion that will emphatically promise that there will *not* be more growth later and that a straight path to destitute poverty will be the only outcome of accepting the student loan usurer's gracious "help."

  We are finally in a position to return to the cryptic claim near the beginning of the present work that the levels of meaning do not present, say, five different objects, just as Aristotle's ten categories did not present ten different objects but rather ten different headings under which one and the same object could be validly considered on rational grounds. In Aristotle's understanding of the categories, to say that an axe is 31 inches long (the category of Quantity), that the axe is brown (the category of Quality), and that it is located in a forest in Canada (the category of Place) are not three distinct objects in addition to the plain designation of the axe in itself without further determination (the category of Substance). One is fundamentally mistaken about the nature of categories if one does not see that at any level within the hierarchy one is still really talking about the same substance. The axe as "an axe located in a forest in Canada" clearly is the same substance of the axe as one would find any of the other categories, including the deepest category of substance. The axe located in a forest in Canada is simply the same axe evaluated within a higher order register in which the standard of meaning is place rather than quality, quantity, or substance as such. Substance is peculiar, therefore, in that it travels into the higher order categories without making them categories of substance per se.

Similarly, the following table does not enumerate five different objects. Each layer is merely a different manifestation of the same underlying resource: fossil fuels. Modern usury is, quite literally, just a euphemism for or half-understood glimpse into fossil fuels. One difference between the following layers, though, is that each higher level in the following table implicitly contains its predecessors. The system of Economics which provides the systematic rationale for usury can only "make sense" if it implicitly contains the lower levels of the sense object of a loan, a deep meme distorting consciousness to hold a shape of linear progress, and the Soma of fossil fuels. Likewise, dwelling at the default level of Mythology implicitly contains all the lower levels, though each lower meaning is obfuscated unless explicitly viewed from its own layer. The following table demonstrates how each higher level implies or contains each lower layer:
[3]

| Layer | Example | Minimal Unit of Meaning |
|---|---|---|
| Soma | Fossil Fuels | Presence |
| Deep Meme | Linear Progress | Shape |
| Sense Object | Student Loan | Form |
| System | Economics | Value |
| Mythology | American Dream | Event |

*Bicycling through Decline*

This hierarchy of structures is not unique to the era of Fossil Fuels, such that everything elaborated in this book will only be applicable to the brief period of human history which is ending as the author writes these words. One could even restore this order of meanings to the prehistoric woolly mammoth hunters who trekked the vast wildernesses of North America long before the bloodthirsty thief Columbus "discovered" anything:

[4]

| Layer | Example | Minimal Unit of Meaning |
|---|---|---|
| Soma | Mammoth Herds | Presence |
| Deep Meme | Level Plane | Shape |
| Sense Object | Hunting Spear | Form |
| System | Systems of Tracking for Herd Movements | Value |
| Mythology | Animistic Spirituality | Event |

One may object to the inclusion of a Gnostic Layer in the Ice Age, perhaps on the assumption that woolly mammoth hunters were too primitive to deal with systems. Such a person would fail to see the irony that modern scientific and mathematical systems are merely a subspecies of prehistoric animal tracking systems which, in a certain sense, embody a more purified example of system than any of the prestigious endeavours which our Priesthood of Progress is so overpaid to pursue. Even the act of reading this text is an instance of the prehistoric ability to coordinate hunting activities on the basis of interpreting the inscriptions left behind by animals and incorporate these traces into a holistic system oriented towards moving in for the kill. In its most purified form, system is not an absolute, transcendent set of objective truths: it is merely a secondary and incomplete glimpse into the woolly mammoth herds which made up its real somatic substance.

One could also speculate about how this hierarchy of five layers will manifest itself in the Post-Oil era of Salvage. Assuming that after Fossil Fuels the world will immediately revert back to an agrarian worldview characteristic of the Middle Ages or a hunter gatherer worldview characteristic of prehistoric times is an understandable first reaction, but it is much more reasonable to predict that the following era will be as unprecedented somatically and memologically as the Fossil Fuel era was. In fact, the era of Salvage will largely just consist of dwelling in the midst of the ghosts of the preceding era of Fossil Fuel Industrialism, in that even without fuel to power the machines, skyscrapers, and industrial products of that era, many of these items will remain within the world as ruins, garbage, or archaic curiosities. However, to say that they will "remain" is complicated by the fact that their lingering presence will entail a transformation of their very essence into a set of different items, reiterating the somatic presence of salvage materials rather than fossil fuels and reiterating the memological shape of a bell curve of decline rather than the memological shape of an ascending ray of progress. The objects, systems, and myths that emerge out of these foundational somatic and memological layers will therefore change the very meaning of what these items are but this change will not be random or senseless but will follow from the influence of living in an era of ruins which will be repurposed to meet needs unimaginable to the engineers who built this infrastructure on the assumption that the fuel to run them would never run out.

The author would propose that one sense object that will be vitally important in the coming era of Salvage will be the bicycle. Although bicycles obviously exist in the era of Fossil Fuels, they are largely seen as an exercise tool or, at worst, a recreational pastime. In fact, Dmitry Orlov has noted that those who find themselves forced to start commuting to work by bicycle in the near future may be dismayed to find that the bicycles available in their local area could more properly be described as cheap toys than as serious means of transportation.[36] Regardless of their current

---

[36] "The most successful form of transportation by far is the bicycle. While there is currently a bicycle for almost every person in the US, these bicycles by and large sit still in garages and basements, rusting and gathering dust. About a tenth of them might be rideable at any given time. If large numbers of people attempt to start using them, the immediate effect will be a shortage of bicycle tires, which deteriorate due to dry rot. Even if this problem finds a solution, it will soon be discovered that the vast majority of the bicycles are in fact toys designed for sport, not for hauling loads or for the rigors of a daily commute, and most of them will fail within a year of hard daily use. Overhauling them requires a wide

neglect, bicycles are still the most efficient means of transportation ever invented and will be prized as vital tools in an impoverished future in which the only other options include walking and riding horses (which entail heavy feeding costs.) John Michael Greer has gone as far as to speculate that bicycles might provide an important military advantage in the wars of the far future, in which the party that escapes by bicycle after an ambush might have a significant enough advantage to win a battle.

Bicycles embody the Salvage Worldview in that, like the skyscraper ruins that will line the horizon amidst urban vacant lots repurposed to hold goats or small fields of wheat, bicycles will linger long after no one is able to actually produce them. Bicycles obviously have far more modest manufacturing requirements than cars or trucks, yet they are still beyond the scope of what even the best Ancient Greek blacksmiths could produce with the hammer, forge, anvil, and other simple tools which the blacksmiths of the far future will also be limited to. Bicycles therefore embody the worldview of preserving a relic that cannot be reproduced but which can be maintained.

As sense objects, bicycles will also provide the basis for systems of knowledge and mythologies to develop. The system of post-industrial calibration, in which repairing an existing bicycle will take precedence over buying a new one (which eventually won't be an option anyway), will provide the most important general system of knowledge in an era in which scientific arcana will be either too expensive to continue pursuing or simply irrelevant to the daily needs of a population largely consumed in the tasks of slaughtering pigs, milking the neighbourhood cattle, and

---

assortment of imported spare parts, which is unlikely to be available. The old three-speed Columbias and other antiques, which were designed to carry 300 pounds and to go 100,000 miles between overhauls, will suddenly become highly prized. Many other bikes will still be used, even if they are no longer rideable, as push-bikes, Ho Chi Minh Trail style: they will be walked instead of ridden, with one stick shoved down the seat-post, another tied to the handlebar and heavy loads slung in bags over the top tube."
 Orlov, Dmitry, *Reinventing Collapse: The Soviet Experience and American Prospects*, (Gabriola Island: New Society Publishers, 2011).

harvesting vegetables from the urban vacant lot gardens. In addition, a mythology in which physical exertion to power a bicycle is literally seen as a religious virtue against the vice of lazily sitting in a car will provide the general moral framework for an elaborate folklore depicting the wickedness of past generations of drivers. Extant Nascar race tracks in North Carolina and New Hampshire will likely serve the same imaginative role that the Coliseum provided for medieval Christians who castigated the wickedness of Roman blood sport against the ascetic virtue of the Medieval Era. In the case of Nascar the main evil on display will be the callous disregard for wasting countless gallons of oil just to drive around in circles for hours.
[5]

| Layer | Example | Minimal Unit of Meaning |
| --- | --- | --- |
| Soma | Salvage | Presence |
| Deep Meme | Bell Curve | Shape |
| Sense Object | Bicycle | Form |
| System | Post-Industrial Calibration | Value |
| Mythology | "Nascar Track is symbol of evil" | Event |

*Why Oil?*

Before delving any deeper into the obscure territory of Philosophy, a small sample of the deeply-disturbing empirical data on our situation will be necessary to avoid pursuing this Philosophy at a level of abstraction so vague as to be useless. In the Peak Oil Literature genre, it is customary to provide some numbers to explicate just how lethally-dependent we have become upon fossil fuels. The previously-mentioned 23,200 hours of human labour contained in one barrel of oil is more "stored work" than one human could accomplish in a full year of working over 40 hours per week, in which case the total would come out to less than a quarter of this amount.[37] Yet each day, some 94 million barrels (or 3,948,000,000 gallons) are consumed worldwide, an extraordinary amount of energy expended just to keep a mostly unsatisfying and grotesquely unjust society churning along for one more day; worse still, this Herculean accomplishment will go unnoticed by virtually anyone, as the vast majority of the citizens of modernity will have wasted that entire day glued to smartphone screens, chugging soda pop, and following tabloid news on Kim Kardashian. The numerical figure for how many hours of stored human labour are burned every single day is so large as to be representable only in scientific notation: $2.1808e+12$. It is even more difficult to conceptualize that this gargantuan amount of energy from petroleum still only amounts to some 33% of the total energy consumption worldwide. Petroleum is indeed the Memological Symbol of all Fossil Fuels, but it is far from the only contributor to this massive supply of stored labour so cluelessly squandered each day.

Few citizens of the United States realize the extent to which they personally benefit from this arrangement. Even those disenfranchised by an economic system rigged to support the well-to-do through artificially propping up a national housing bubble, the student loan scam, a diploma mill university system, and a bogus stock market are not completely left out of this system of free energy stolen from hundreds of millions of years of geological processes. The average American has over 200 energy slaves at his or her disposal to accomplish work which will eventually have to be shoved back onto the hands of the slave owner, a fate to be avoided only by those Americans in the future who are morally-bankrupt enough to resort to coercing real human slaves to fill this void.[38]

---

[37] This figure is even harder to understand for the millions of Americans who don't even lift anything heavier than a cup of coffee at "work" in their air-conditioned offices. Obviously here the author means hard, physically-demanding labour.

[38] Dmitry Orlov gives a particular memorable summary of the unspoken slave economy in modernity: "Currently, the value of money and other tokens of wealth, such as gold coins, is amplified by fossil fuel energy providing a replacement for human and animal labor equivalent to hundreds of personal slaves for each American . . . When this fossil fuel energy is no longer available,

Nothing is more embarrassing to humans' innate rationality than the standard of discourse on the topic of fossil fuel depletion. Public responses waver among several predictable responses, yet even the most superficially "informed" of these still displays astonishing ignorance of the numerical impossibility of replacing the sublime amount of stored ἔργον[39] so casually wasted to power just one more day of four hour commutes, playing virtual Solitaire on the company computer, idling one's car while waiting in line to grab a paper bag full of pseudo-food from a drive-thru window, and vegetating to state-controlled talking heads after a long day of "working hard" warming an office chair.

First, as was already mentioned, appealing to "technological innovation" to solve the problem of Peak Oil misrecognizes that the problem of resource depletion is itself caused by too many machines' burning finite reserves of fossil fuels out of existence. Prescribing more "technological innovation" (a mere euphemism for building more machines) is therefore literally akin to attempting to treat a patient for alcohol poisoning by giving him more vodka.

On the other hand, appeals to so-called "Green Energy" sources make a slightly more subtle error that still fundamentally misunderstands the role of fossil fuels. The politically correct fantasy of "elevating" all 7 billion residents of the Earth into a universal suburban, college-educated, office drone middle class while simultaneously expressing nominal concern about the climate change which is the unavoidable consequence of those same historically-unprecedented lifestyles can only be resolved through the presumed existence of some Clean Energy source that will allow the same lifestyle to be achieved without any of the hypocrisy or guilt that currently factor into so blatant a contradiction. The inconvenient fact that no such energy source has ever been proven

---

no personal slaves will suddenly materialize out of nowhere and be willing to work for a few pennies a day, because these pennies, in turn, will buy nothing." Ibid.

[39] The author prefers the Ancient Greek term "ἔργον" to the ambiguous Modern English word "work," given that so much of what passes as "work" by the standards of the Modern American Economy is a laughable caricature of the kind of serious, hard labor that was once performed by everyone except kings.

to exist does not stop the Clean Energy activists from claiming somehow to be proponents of a scientific positivism which would render alternative models of the future indefensible.

Despite ample funding and decades of research, no such source has ever yet emerged that can produce even a tiny fraction of the net energy gained from the fossil fuel sources, let alone meet expectations that the Clean Energy future would be even more prosperous than our current Fossil Fuel Industrial Civilization. After all, no one yelling about the need to dump more government subsidies into Clean Energy companies does so with the assumption that the resulting "Green Civilization" would be any less materially prosperous than the current Fossil Fuel Civilization they claim to renounce. Such a person certainly isn't envisioning a world in which personal cars, air conditioning, hot showers, and a 24/7 internet connection are not still available for a reasonable price and at any time one happens to desire them. This presumed society is certainly imagined to be one still filled with suburbs or, perhaps, a universalized Manhattan copied and pasted over the entire globe, in which pedestrians stroll down well-lit avenues lined with fancy shops and lively night clubs amidst the traffic of streets packed with buses, taxis, and luxury cars. The Elon Musk Frenzy has taken this fantasy to an even more absurd level: our era is arguably the only one in history in which one of the world's supposedly "most brilliant minds" has responded to the problem of mounting pollution and declining resources on the Earthy by proposing to relocate to Mars, a task which, even if it could be carried out, would impose a hefty amount of pollution and resource depletion in its own right. Yet the enthusiasts who get behind this plan are most definitely not planning to live in a Martian colony that is *not* made in the image of their favorite urban or suburban community on the Earth now. If they were told they might have to accept living more like a lower class peasant on the desert planet of Arrakis from *Dune*, it would be difficult to imagine their enthusiasm remaining so delusionally high. In either case, the "Clean Energy" activists' vision of the future is most definitely *not* one of mud huts which lack electricity, running water, central heating, and an internet connection or a remote rural village in which peasants stake out a difficult existence on the basis of tending sheep, planting potatoes, and blacksmithing tools from salvaged metal. The fact that life expectancy and infant mortality rates in such a context will return to levels familiar in the Medieval Era is another factor that will be left unconsidered even by those who claim to have thought out the problem of the Post-Oil Future the most thoroughly.

It is entirely questionable whether the so-called Clean Energy sources really are energy sources at all: John Michael Greer has repeatedly noted that solar panels, for example, require sophisticated manufacturing processes and rare physical components (which, in turn, require global shipping networks) in order to be produced. The total energy bill to assemble a single functioning solar panel is therefore only about equal to the total amount of solar energy it will produce in its lifetime before requiring maintenance or replacement. Therefore, the solar panel is not really an energy source so much as it is a storage mechanism by which the energy invested into its manufacturing is released a little bit at a time at a later date.

What is all too easy to miss is that this energy which a solar panel effectively stores did not originally come from solar panels. Solar panels fall prey to the paradox of recursion: it is not possible to generate solar panels from solar panels. It is arguably a misnomer to even call solar panels "renewable" because the problem of recursion is not a problem for genuinely renewable natural resources. Rabbits, for example, do not suffer from the paradox of recursion. Rabbits can reproduce rabbits without any trouble; in fact, stopping them from doing so would pose the greater challenge. Sheep also tend to reproduce other sheep without issue, but of course sheep and rabbits are not the kind of renewable resources upon which a universal class of suburban idlers could be based. The problem of recursion is therefore a far more reliable measure for how valid or how illusory a claim to renewability is than any of the willfully dishonest measures which the media and academic industry currently provide.

Rather than a closed circle of natural sustainability, the so-called Clean Energy scams merely emerge secondarily from a definite external origin which is of a decidedly non-renewable nature. Ultimately, somewhere in the genealogy of a solar panel one will find a hidden subsidy which fossil fuel sources provided, without which the solar panel would have been simply far too sophisticated and energy-intensive to produce. In other words, solar panels are not an alternative to fossil fuels at all. The very word "solar panel" is just a half-understood euphemism for fossil fuels; a solar panel is just a counter sense object founded upon the Soma of petroleum, as it is an "energy source" that just doesn't happen to actually produce any energy. Doing justice to this hierarchy of truthfulness in which an unclear or intentionally-misleading euphemism is subordinated to its underlying Truth will require a revision of the very notion of Truth, a task which the Peak Oil Movement cannot accomplish without falling into the obscure territory of Philosophy.

## *Euphemism or Epiphenomenon?*

The author's emphasis on euphemism implies a relation between the unclear and the clear, between the imperfect and the perfect, between half-truth and truth, and between less being and more being. Yet in a Post-Metaphysical Era in which it is not even clear what it means to have any being at all, it is certainly unclear what it would mean to have "more being." Likewise, the present text will reawaken the Heideggerian quest for an interrogation of Being qua Being through formulating a unique Fundamental Ontology of Limitation crafted through an honest response to the reality of Peak Oil and its transcendental implications for past and future eras' own relations to crucial resources for survival.

The present text will therefore present something of a transcendental critique of the Phenomenological structures by which meaning is disclosed within a historically contingent horizon of dwelling, yet the result will not be satisfactorily obtained through simply applying the results of Heidegger's *Being and Time*, or any other established philosophy, to the problem of Peak Oil. Rather, the author shall propose that Heidegger's emphasis on the primordial existential structures of Dasein, although enormously beneficial to this project, will not in itself be sufficient to grasp the extent to which the era of Fossil Fuel Modernity has come to embody transcendental structures of meaningfulness which are utterly incompatible with those that characterized the Hunter Gatherer and Agrarian eras of the past, as well as those that will characterize the future Post-Oil era of Salvage. A more or less uniform analysis of Dasein's fundamental characteristics will be supplanted by a critique of the shift in foundations which occurred in the transition from horizons of awareness disclosed within Hunter Gatherer to Agrarian to Fossil Fuel to Salvage eras, a shift which is not a transition to a new Pseudo-Marxist "mode of production" but rather to a different underlying substance, a substance upon which even Heidegger's disclosure of a horizon of hermeneutical meaning is founded.

The author will challenge Heidegger by claiming that the substance of Fossil Fuel's presence is the basis upon which what Heidegger called *Lichtung* (the German word for "clearing") is revealed. This claim will of course shock readers familiar with Heidegger's *Being and Time* for the following reasons which deserve to be discussed briefly before proceeding. Heidegger favoured describing Dasein (Existence, roughly) through the metaphor of a disclosed clearing in the woods but was careful to note that Dasein is not just the objects in the clearing: Dasein *is* its own clearing.[40] Traditional Metaphysics used abstractly-purified physical objectivity as a theoretical model from which to derive the categories of all beings and in turn to generate an understating of Being itself; the primary category was, of course, substance, since any object that had a higher order category instantiated in it such as a quality (i.e., to be coloured red) or a location (i.e., to be in New Delhi, India) could only have those higher order categorical features if it already existed as a substance.[41] Heidegger revolutionized Ontology by revealing instead that the substantial core of an object was not a universal framework for understanding Being qua Being, since any substance inferred from a "present object" was just an

---

[40] Heidegger, Martin. *Being and Time* Trans. Joan Stambaugh (Albany: State University of New York Press, 1996), p. 125.
[41] Aristotle, *The Physics*, in *Basic Works of Aristotle* (New York: The Modern Library, 2002), p. 223.

abstraction away from Dasein's more primordial stance of Being-in-the-World. Certainly, an object could be encountered as something present at hand (*Vorhandenheit*) if one simply stared at it to explicitly catalogue its attributes under the traditional categorical headings; but this was only possible because Dasein was already involved with that object as, say, a tool which was made available to Dasein for use within a totality of equipment ready at hand (*Zuhandenheit*). If one had encountered a hammer as a hammer, for example, that was only because the totality of woodworking tools for a certain project was already given as a totality before the hammer was encountered as a single tool.[42] Likewise, there was no need to determine whether the object really existed or whether it was just an empty appearance in one's mind, because Dasein was always already out there in the world rather than trapped in the interior box of a subjective stream of consciousness.

On the basis of these revelations, Heidegger concluded that substance cannot be the deepest layer of an absolute hierarchy of categories of Being because substance is itself founded upon a set of more fundamental structures: one can only gain a notion of substantiality if one has obtained it from an interpretation, specifically an interpretation oriented towards the innerworldly beings, or the things in Dasein's disclosed world. But these innerworldly beings had to first be discovered. If they were discovered, that means that they were discovered as things taken care of by Dasein within a revealed world. Understanding is therefore more primordial than substance and is a foundation which is gravely distorted by traditional Metaphysics' tendency to ground the absolute notion of Being in some obscure idea of objective substance. Without Dasein's understanding, substance would be meaningless as a concept because the very act of perception by which the object was stared at had to already have been founded upon an interpretation of the object as "a something" rather than as so much brute matter.[43] Encountering a hammer "as a hammer" rather than as an anonymous blob of colours and tactile sensations

---

[42] Heidegger, Martin. *Being and Time* Trans. Joan Stambaugh (Albany: State University of New York Press, 1996), p. 64.
[43] Ibid., p. 187.

required that this perception be founded upon understanding. One certainly could abstract a category of substance away from an act of staring at the hammer as an isolated object, but misreading this substantiality for the definition of Being qua Being was an error that could no longer be conceivable after Heidegger.

How, then, could the author of the present volume possibly suggest that we return to a Metaphysics of Substance by speaking of the Soma of Transcendental Oil as the substance of the modern worldview? The author accepts Heidegger's argument that objectivity is founded upon more primordial structures than itself, yet the author's own use of the term "substance" must not be equivocated with any common-sense notion of objectivity. After all, counter sense objects have a role in the author's system as well but the counter sense object is not the Soma; it is itself just a higher order content which must be founded on the Soma in order to be given.

It is debatable, in fact, whether even the Ancient Greek thinkers Plato and Aristotle who pioneered the original tradition of a Philosophy of Substance and Essence understood substance as a mystical object hidden behind its appearances. In Book 4 of Aristotle's *Metaphysics,* for example, he argues that substance is not an objective, inaccessible material base underlying the attributes accessible to perception on the surface level but is instead something like an *a priori* structure which can be justified on rational grounds alone in order to avoid the paradox of infinite recursion. The following quote summarizes this dilemma:

> But if *all* statements are accidental, there will be nothing primary about which they are made, if the accidental always implies predication about a subject. The predication, then, must go on *ad infinitum*. But this is impossible; for not even two terms can be combined in an accidental predication. For an accident is not an accident of an accident, unless it be because both are accidents of the same substance.[44]

---

[44] Aristotle, *The Metaphysics* In *Basic Works of Aristotle* (New York: The Modern Library, 2001), p. 740.

The author has no need to extrapolate beyond Aristotle's own words to make this connection between substance and the epistemological limit of knowledge, as Aristotle quite literally provided this definition himself in his dictionary of terms in Book V of *The Metaphysics*:

> 'Limit' means . . . the substance of each thing, and the essence of each; for this is the limit of knowledge; and if of knowledge, of the object also.[45]

In Book V of *The Physics*, Aristotle similarly notes that change can only occur in a subject, for speaking of a motion undergoing motion would lead to an infinite regress which would logically prevent any determinate change from being accomplished from start to finish:

> [I]f there is to be change of change and becoming of becoming, we shall have an infinite regress . . . And since in an infinite series there is no first term, here will be no first stage and therefore no following stage either. On this hypothesis then nothing can become or be moved or changed.[46]

In Plato's dialogue *Theaetetus*, the title character also poses the question whether a logical error has been committed in attempting to define the fundamental structures in terms of more fundamental structures:

> But how can anyone, Socrates, tell the elements of an element? . . . [They] may be the most truly said to be undefined.[47]

---

[45] Ibid., p. 770.
[46] Aristotle, *The Physics* In *Basic Works of Aristotle* (New York: The Modern Library, 2001), p. 304.
[47] Plato, *The Theaetetus*, in *Collected Dialogues* (Princeton: Princeton University Press, 1989).

A similar dialogue occurs in Plato's *Cratylus* as the characters search for the foundations of a purified language, a language in which each thing's "true name" could reflect its eternal essence in the medium of language:

> But if we take a word which is incapable of further resolution, then we shall be right in saying that we have at last reached a primary element, which need not be resolved any further.[48]

These texts from Plato and Aristotle demonstrate that in Ancient Greek Metaphysics a foundation is not a mystical superstition thought to dwell behind the set of visible attributes; a foundation is simply that which has no deeper foundation than itself, for to ask for the foundation of a foundation is to misunderstand the very meaning of this term. The Metaphysics of Objectivity critiqued by Heidegger has no intrinsic relation to substance considered as a limit on recursion or as a foundational structure upon which other structures such as memological shape, objective sense, systematic value, and mythological event are founded, as the remainder of the present volume shall explain in great detail: a limit is not an object at all, for one only gets the notion of an object by implicitly working from the Metaphysical foundation provided by Limitation itself.

Given this understanding of substance as the limit to recursion rather than an objective entity behind the set of phenomenal appearances, the author shall argue that in our era it is the substance of fossil fuels, not Dasein, that discloses the foundational horizon of meaningfulness upon which all the shallower horizons of meaning are founded. Other transcendental registers of meaning, such as Mythology, System, Objectivity, and Memology are higher order structures which are intelligible only insofar as they are founded upon the more primordial dimension of this substance.

---

[48] Plato, Plato, *The Cratylus*, in *Collected Dialogues* (Princeton: Princeton University Press, 1989), p. 459.

Substance provides the deepest layer to a hierarchy of meanings insofar as substance acts as a singular limit to the infinitely recursive variation possible at higher order levels of meaning: the number of different possible myths is theoretically infinite, just as systems' ability to expand linearly has manifested itself in a number of Mathematical systems devoted quite literally to the different varieties of infinity. Likewise, substance cannot be interpreted through the rational criteria unique to the higher layers founded upon it. Substance cannot be grasped as a mythological event, a systematic value, an objective entity, or even a memological shape. The sole rational criteria proper to substance is presence, though the author means something rather different by that word than the kind of presence so vehemently attacked by Heidegger and the schools of Deconstrustivist and Postmodernist Theory which he inspired. The present volume therefore cannot rely on an application of any pre-existent Philosophy to the problem of Peak Oil. Rather than produce a "Heideggerian critique of Peak Oil," for example, the present volume shall develop an original "Peak Oil Philosophy."

The kind of Peak Oil Philosophy needed to move beyond this blindness to the unspoken substance behind a network of surface-level epiphenomena may offend a reader sufficiently familiar with Philosophy's legacy as a universal science, in that a properly universal analysis of Being should be irreducible to any single empirical concern like geological rates of petroleum extraction. Although Peak Oil certainly is a geological problem built upon the hard physical limits of petroleum production and extraction which *no* amount of political, technological, financial, or scientific tinkering can override, it would be wrong to think of Peak Oil Philosophy as just some perverse "Geological Philosophy," a term as inappropriate as "Botanical Philosophy" or "Zoological Philosophy." Peak Oil Philosophy is not some monstrosity that would attempt to found the universal and transcendental science of Philosophy on the tiny island of one geological concern, a project which any thinker familiar with the notion of Fundamental Ontology would find objectionable and deeply flawed. Rather, Peak Oil Philosophy is arguably the *only* honest philosophy which can be formulated in light of the revelation that the planet already reached its peak of petroleum production in the year 2005 and has embarked on the downhill slope of depletion ever since, evidenced by the global financial crisis of 2008 and the bleak historical events of resource wars, regime changes, mass migrations, waves of populist backlash, crashing standards of living, international debt crises, and growing economic chaos around the globe ever since. Yet Peak Oil Philosophy can also legitimately claim to be a Universal Philosophy in that Peak Oil is something of a transcendental gateway to understand the generalized structures by which crucial resource bases such as fossil fuels in modernity, agrarian grain in the Medieval and Ancient eras, or herds of megafauna in the Ice Age and prehistoric eras come to occupy the deepest position within a hierarchy of levels of intelligibility which dominate even our prized systems and mythologies. In our era, below a sprawling set of surface-level constructs of meaning lies nothing more than a single, immensely powerful but quickly vanishing substance: *everything we do is a euphemism for burning fossil fuels.*

### *Salvaging Truth: Plato, Russell, Haag*

The author therefore does not favour a Postmodern or Deconstructivist rejection of rigid divisions between truth and falsity or even a rejection of distinctions between greater and lesser degrees of truth. In fact, the present text seeks to continue the long-abandoned tradition of a seeking a schema by which to move from imperfect half-truths to perfect full-truths. Bertrand Russell made the last great attempt at this archaic project by constructing an ideal super-language that removed the possibility of "ambiguity" and "misleading language" which had plagued ordinary discourse; he did so by providing a schema by which unclear statements in natural language could be translated into perfectly clear statements in logical symbolic notation.[49] Despite considerable methodological disagreements with Ancient Greek Philosophy, Russell's movement from imperfection to perfection at the level of truth and clarity

---

[49] Russell, Bertrand, *Principles of Mathematics* (London: Routledge, 2012), p xxxvii.

should not be thought of as a contradiction of Plato's original attempt to do the same thing. In fact, the most notable difference between Plato and Russell is just that Plato assumed this could be accomplished in the medium of intuition, especially the perfect intuition of ideal objects which a disembodied soul that had fled the body after death could behold directly in the Realm of Ideas, while Russell sought to achieve this in the medium of a perfect syntactic system capable of accounting for both the logically-clarified content of statements rendered in natural language and for the axiomatic logical basis of Peano Arithmetic and higher forms of Mathematics.

Russell devised a gnostic system in which truth values were yielded from strings of symbolic values ordered correctly by a sophisticated logical syntax and secured by the foundations of a small set of undefinable symbols which provided the basis for the definition of other values.[50] Interestingly, Russell did not see any need to ground the systematic ambiguity of Natural Language in some foundation which was non-systematic in nature: rather, he sought out a clearer logical system in which he could ground the systems of Natural Language, Mathematics, and even Philosophy.[51]

Russell's main error, therefore, lay in assuming that the imperfections of the established gnostic systems could be resolved by generating a perfect system that still remained within the gnostic register of meaning; this was because he assumed no other non-gnostic register really existed because even things that seemed to lie outside the reach of systems were really systematic values in disguise.[52] Russell's Metaphysics favoured gnostic systematicity to

---

[50] In Russell's *Principles of Mathematics*, for example, implication was undefinable in terms of other operators precisely because those other operators were definable in terms of implication
Ibid., p. 15.

[51] "[P]ure mathematics must contain no indefinables except logical constants, and consequently no premises, or indemonstrable propositions, but such as are concerned exclusively with logical constants and with variables . . . The logical constants themselves are to be defined only by enumeration, for they are so fundamental that all the properties by which the class of them might be defined presuppose some terms of the class."
Ibid., p. 8.

[52] Just a few of the gnostic systems which Russell analysed include Natural

the exclusion of other registers. For example, he used the famous example of Piccadilly in London to demonstrate that what appeared to be a thing was really a systematic construct. Piccadilly in London only appears to be a single entity due to linguistic ambiguity. In reality, Piccadilly is just a logical class of material objects. Even time loses its status as an object and is instead revealed to be a class of instants. By Russell's later period of thought, "things" disappear as such: natural language misleads one to think he or she is speaking about a thing but he or she is really just saying extraordinarily complicated things about empirical sense contents, using the gnostic resources of a massively-complicated logical system which always underlies the discourse of even the most ignorant speaker. This complication which was obscured in intuition and natural language could, in theory, be rendered transparent in the symbolic notation provided in Russell's mature multi-volume work *Principia Mathematica*.[53]

Of course, Gödel's Incompleteness Theorems largely made Russell's systematic approach to this task seem unthinkable by revealing that any formal system sufficiently powerful to provide a logical foundation to Peano Arithmetic must contain at least one statement the truth or validity of which cannot be proved by the system, as well as exposing the problem of self-referentiality (a system's inability to make statements about itself.)[54] One should not, however, mistake Gödel's refutation of Russell's systematic and syntactic approach for an adequate refutation of the project towards clarity as originally envisaged by Plato, as Russell and Plato worked in fundamentally different registers of meaning. Gödel's objections are valid only to the extent that one remains within the gnostic register of meaning but Plato did not limit himself to that layer. The author of the present volume will also differ from Russell by showing that any gnostic system, however

---

Language, Euclidian Geometry, Newtonian Physics, and Peano Arithmetic.
Ibid., pp. 54, 405, 489, 10.
[53] Russell, Bertrand and Alfred North Whitehead, *Principia Mathematica*. Vol. 1. (Lexington: Rough Draft Printing, 1910).

[54] Hofstadter, Douglas. *Gödel Escher Bach* (New York: Vintage, 1980), p. 53.

seemingly perfect, is still ultimately founded upon the deeper layers of sense objectivity, memology, and somatic presence, levels which Russell was beholden to even in his disregard for their very existence. Russell's own system was merely a sprawling reiteration of a certain way of viewing the world which could be manifested much better in a single object, the object of a thinking machine. The counter sense object of a thinking machine states more clearly in a single glance what Russell stated much more unclearly in over 60 books and over 2,000 articles, despite trying to be the philosopher of clarity *par excellence*!

Unlike Russell, Plato did not conceive of the movement from imperfect to perfect truth to be a matter of systematic value bound by the grammar of well-formed strings. Rather, In Plato's Realm of Ideas one gained the full truth by seeing it, but one did not see (or more precisely, one did not *read*) sentences written out with words or any other type of gnostic values expressed in symbolic notation. What one saw in Plato's Realm of Ideas were intuitive manifestations of Truth given in a level of Phenomenological purity inaccessible even to the most perceptive embodied person. Plato's Realm of Ideas was a space populated by Forms that embodied their essences through unambiguous morphological specificity; it was *not* a gallery of perfectly-constructed strings of symbols of linguistic sentences. The transcendental register of intelligible form, whether as geometrical abstraction or as concrete object (Plato wavers between the two), cannot be reduced to the transcendental register of systematic value which Russell preferred.

In principle, the author does not disagree with Plato's approach to uncovering finer grades of truthfulness or even with Russell's belief that unclear statements could be replaced by clear statements through developing a highly-refined methodology. Yet the author will differ from both in that neither systems nor sense objects make up the deepest foundation upon which both are founded and from which both gain their intelligibility. Rather, mythological, systematic, sense objective, and memological meanings are all founded upon the deepest layer of raw presence, the raw presence of a Soma which manifests its existence in a medium more fundamental even than a visual image given to sight.

In our era, the presence of Fossil Fuels are the unspoken foundation upon which claims of systematic intelligibility and objective sense are based. The movement from an unsatisfactorily-clear systematic statement to a clearer objective sense could therefore be carried even further, terminating at the deepest level of arriving at the existence of the Fossil Fuels whose presence is a higher truth than could be captured in any of the higher order layers that inhere within it. We are living in an era of transition, however, in which that presence is beginning to dim and the era of absence is drawing near. The loss of this base will not merely result in the loss of truth for all the Soma as a present body, although that certainly will be a huge problem in its own right. The loss of the Soma's presence will also mean a loss of being for the myths, systems, objects and memes which only had as much being as they could borrow from the Soma.

This relation between Truth and Being will likely offend modern rationalist sensibilities but a very serious case could be made for a return to Plato's idiosyncratic understanding of the problem. It would perhaps seem impossible to revive Plato's dualistic Philosophy of Truth in a modern world, yet Plato's hope for such a hierarchical ordering by which one could proceed from imperfect truth to perfect truth by moving allegorically from shadows on a wall to the true things of which they were mere imitations is not a model of truth with which the author has any intrinsic disagreement. In fact, the author even agrees with Plato's highly-controversial view that this movement up the latter to higher levels of truth was simultaneously a movement up the latter to higher levels of being, as Martin Heidegger noted in his lectures on the Allegory of the Cave in Plato's *Republic*:

> [H]e who removes the shackles, says that what is now revealed . . . the things themselves and the human beings, are μᾶλλον ὄντα, *are* to a greater degree [*mehr seined*], are *more beingful* [seiender] beings. What *is* admits of degrees![55]

---

[55]Heidegger, Martin, *The Essence of Truth* (London: Bloomsbury: 2002), p. 29.

Moving from a vague euphemism like "technological innovation" to its true content as an imperfect manifestation of Fossil Fuels is similarly a movement from less being to more being. It is not that these abstractions have no being at all or that they are mere illusions: it is rather that they only have being insofar as they borrow being from the true source of which they are a mere euphemism. A solar panel is a counter sense object promising to power the entire world while being incapable even of producing other solar panels like itself; yet it would be incorrect to claim that this object which embodies paradox in its very essence has no being at all or that it is sheer falsity. It is rather just a distorted manifestation of fossil fuels, an incomplete symbol less beingful than the true Soma from which it borrowed what little being it has.

*Peak Oil Philosophy's Hour*

Clearly, the time has come for a fully-developed, serious Peak Oil Philosophy to supplement the body of Peak Oil Literature written thus far which has never ventured as deep into the obscure realm of Philosophy as the present text. No intellectually-honest response to the problem of a dualism between an underlying fossil fuel resource and the dysfunctional Mythology of Progress which is literally killing the Earth (and increasingly, all of the humans upon it) can treat this problem satisfactorily without developing some Peak Oil Philosophy, however implicit or vague. The life or death seriousness of the issue will also liberate the present discussion to renew ideas long banished from the academy in favour of more "fashionable" theories, the value of which was measured more by the bubble economics of a rising stock value than by the classical standard of enduring credibility. The present discussion cannot afford to be beholden to intellectual fads such as Marxism, Psychoanalysis, Queer Theory, Postcolonialism, Neurplasticity, or Social Justice Politics which are certain to not survive the coming mass closure of universities in the wake of the decline of the student loan bubble, the international currency crisis, skyrocketing energy prices, and the inevitable transition to a Post-Peak Oil World.

In conclusion of this chapter, it is important to note that the present text is largely a response to the author's own frustration from *not* being able to find a book like the present over many years. Perhaps like the Science Fiction archetype of a man who cannot find the "perfect woman" who exactly embodies some bizarre private fantasy and then responds to this absence by simply inventing the perfect woman himself, the author has decided to write the present volume rather than wait for a text which is overwhelmingly unlikely to emerge from either the Peak Oil or the Philosophy printing presses.

In *The Blood of the Earth*, John Michael Greer noted that those within the Peak Oil Community who are sceptical of the usefulness of incorporating Magic into the discussion should be made aware that their own personal discovery of Peak Oil was literally an example of a magical ritual of initiation.[56] It is not at all clear why only a certain percentage of people to whom the theory is exposed will be able to "see the truth" in the theory, while the vast majority of their colleagues shrug it off with well-known thoughtstoppers like, "They'll think of something." Only a tiny handful will, for no explicable reason, react to Peak Oil by realizing that the entire World of Meanings which was just a moment before taken for granted so casually is on the verge of dissolving into nothingness. The author's own experience of transitioning from dismissing Peak Oil as nonsense to realizing that all of his own expectations about the future would be destroyed by it was a deeply-traumatic experience that required years of coping to come to terms with. Like many who undergo this trauma, the author responded by frantically searching for materials to try to gain some perspective or provide some order to the flood of racing thoughts that could not be repressed any longer, but found that honest materials on the topic were extremely rare and that discussing it openly with friends or family was almost certain to be met with blank incomprehension and indifference, if not angry scepticism and furious denunciation. Coming to terms with the death of one's civilization will always entail a certain time period of lingering in

---

[56] Greer, John Michael, *The Blood of the Earth: An Essay on Magic and Peak Oil* (Agawam: Scarlett Imprint, 2012), p. 42.

denial, rage, bargaining, and depression, but the present volume is the author's own personal instantiation of what acceptance might look like, even within the coordinates of a fully-rationalized philosophical theory.

Finally, it has been nearly ten years since the author first encountered Peak Oil while studying Philosophy at the undergraduate level in Greeley, Colorado in the United States in 2010. Although a comparatively large number of the students in the department had intelligence above average, a number of them small enough to be counted on one hand were much too brilliant to pursue the traditional pathway of obtaining a degree to land a comfortable upper middle class office job and then retire on the secure basis of a lifetime of investing into the financial shenanigans currently considered to be "valuable" (although such an easy path was increasingly not even available to the youth of the "Lost Generation" who graduated in 2011 to nothing except an economy deep in recession and to student loan debts towering into the five or six figure range.) Such figures presented a vision of the future radically unlike anything the author had ever considered, one which the author vehemently rejected until it became impossible to argue logically against the simple fact that a lifestyle that requires enormous amounts of fossil fuels to be wasted on a daily basis just to obtain an unsatisfying quality of life would not be sustained after access to fossil fuels radically dropped in the near future.

Our first response was to band together to flee into the forests of Oregon to start an ecovillage, but this quickly devolved into a psychologically-unhealthy cult in which the proposed ecovillage served as little more than an inkblot over which several partisan political ideologies competed to be its "true essence." Needless to say, the project failed and was abandoned in less than two years' time, leaving a legacy of bitterness which took some years to heal. In fact, when the author travelled all the way across the steep Rocky Mountains to visit the old community members who were living in a cave out in the desert one final time in 2016, talk of renewing the project seemed completely unthinkable.

Nature has a fine sense of humour. One grand irony is that Oregon was chosen as the least drought-prone area of the nation in

2010 but suffered a historic drought just a few years later, a testament to the impossibility of escaping the crisis of Peak Oil by engineering a plan to "multiply rabbits on paper," as the film *Jean de Florette* would put it. Yet even if that were not the case, the project of fleeing industrial civilization to watch it burn from the safety of a remote cob house in the woods surrounded by acres of organic gardening space would have been far less ethical than taking up the task of trying to spread awareness among the "ordinary people" which the ecovillage mentality abandons to catastrophic suffering so indifferently and the industrial communities which the ecovillage mentality so selfishly gives up to destruction. The present volume is the outcome of years of reading countless texts in the fields of Philosophy and Peak Oil, among other fields like Religion, History, Political Theory, and Literature. In a certain sense, the present volume has been planned and rethought-out within the private stream of the author's own consciousness ever since 2011 but there is simply no time left to delay the publication of this work. The author is not sure how the remaining years of his life will unfold but as a student loan refugee living "across the imperial borders" in the obscure rural village of Uchakkada, India, he realizes that a long life free from legal, medical, or financial trouble cannot be taken for granted; in fact, one of the first things that a serious acceptance of Peak Oil makes clear is that a long life *of any kind* cannot be taken for granted. Rather than lament being deprived of the long but purposeless life as a mindless consumer which was promised as a guaranteed outcome for every kid who grew up at the end of the 20th Century, the author finds that having to *not* pass away a lifetime in the meaningless ritual of wasteful consumption is a type of liberation to pursue projects that really matter, precisely with the knowledge that one cannot count on living long enough to waste any more time not doing so. Ted Kaczynski expressed a similar sentiment in a memorable passage from the Unabomber Manifesto:

> Besides, we all have to die some time, and it may be better to die fighting for survival, or for a cause, than to live a long but empty and purposeless life.[57]

Likewise, the author hopes to use the present text to commit to record years of discussions on the topics of Peak Oil and Philosophy that have thus far never been written down. Rather than let all of these perspectives die with the author when his own end comes, the present volume will preserve some of this information and hopefully ignite a discussion that generates other texts on Peak Oil Philosophy by writers who, either by choice or necessity, populate the Cimmerian intellectual frontiers outside the locked gates behind which elitist academic careerists only espouse theories that seem to promise them an easy upper middle class lifestyle and a high salary. In contrast with such obviously self-serving and intellectually-dishonest waste, the present text will be the first in a new type of Cimmerian Philosophy which will be uniquely suited to meet the challenges of our era.

---

[57] Kaczynski, Ted, *Industrial Society and its Future.* In *Technological Slavery* (Port Townsend: Feral House, 2010), p. 91.

Chapter Two
The Bastard in the Court:
Cimmerian Philosophy and the Silent Rebellion against the
Academic Aristocracy


*Beyond Respectability*

As the title of the present volume indicates, the author will utilize a hitherto unexplored "Ontology of Limitation" rather than borrow the resources of some established Ontology such as Heideggerian Dasein, Badiouan Set Theory, or Zizekian Dialectical Incompleteness. Though the author acknowledges his own indebtedness to past thinkers on the subject, the precise paradoxes of Peak Oil's notion of "having more Being" and "having less Being" simply cannot be done proper justice while remaining within previously-developed ontologies that did not take this problem as the central target of critique. Still worse, the temptation to take the "easy way out" by simply applying some academically-fashionable but philosophically-questionable theory like Marxism, Psychoanalysis, Gender Performativity, Postcolonialism, or Neuroplasticity to the deadly-serious problem of Peak Oil would be just as harmful as it would be intellectually dishonest. The author's post-academic and non-academic position as an independent philosopher writing from a concrete house in a rural village in India, a village so obscure as to not even have a Wikipedia page, is something of a necessity to do this work without falling prey to the short-sighted pursuit of academic career advancement, which would *a priori* rule out any serious response to Peak Oil in the first place.

Currently-established theoretical approaches are also simply *incapable* of explaining the challenge of restructuring lifestyles fatally dependent upon a disappearing resource without trivializing the serious, life or death implications of Peak Oil into some comical caricature of an ivory tower abstraction not meant to be taken seriously even by the "radical professor" who is interested in critiquing all of capitalism, except of course for the parts that provide his or her uptown condo, international vacations to Europe, casual flights to academic conferences across the North American continent, and corporate stock investments upon which expectations of a financially-secure retirement are based. Such "revolutionary thinkers" hate everything in capitalism, except for everything in capitalism that allows them to pursue a historically anomalous, energy-wasting upper middle class existence on the backs of underpaid adjuncts living in their cars and deeply-indebted college students forced to sell themselves to student loan indentured servitude to somehow cover the soaring $52,000 per year tuition bill which amounts in many cases to nothing more than a "ticket of admission to sit in the presence" of an anointed intellectual from the Priesthood of Progress. The same ivy league elites who scoff at the superstition of traditionalist Roman Catholics in their belief that the uncorrupted bodies of dead saints might hold some miraculous power worthy of a pilgrimage to Spain or Italy are themselves the beneficiaries of a system that sells pilgrimages to the holy sites of Modernity such as Yale and Stanford where the "lucky few" pay exorbitant rates for the hopes of obtaining some miraculous favour to their careers if they can just get a seat in the lecture hall close enough to the circumference of influence radiating from the tenured professors in order to absorb some of the magical power exuding from their "holy bodies."

  A new anti-academic Philosophy is taking root as the author writes these words. This book shall be among its first intellectual offspring. In the legend of the Emperor's New Clothes, the bastard in the court who was liberated to speak the obvious fact that the emperor was butt-naked in plain view of all and that his new clothes were, in fact, nothing at all has a role which every academic careerist shuns like bloody death but which the author celebrates having obtained. Lacking a legitimate father, the bastard was *a priori* ruled out from even having the opportunity to *try* to participate in the self-serving social game of agreeing with lies just to try to advance oneself within the entrenched aristocracy of dishonest yes-men who will literally say *anything* to get a slightly higher position within a parasitic hierarchy of professional idlers who consume the products of the labour of the peasant and craftsman Others outside their gated walls. The author fashions himself something of an intellectual bastard who is also *a priori* excluded from the entire delicate dance of aristocratic social advancement within the academy and, as a proud exile of the diploma mill industry, is free to speak from the frosty, undomesticated steppes of Cimmeria with no regard for the repercussions to a career which the author could not pursue even if he somehow wanted to.

At any rate, a closer look at the fads engulfing the modern American college campuses in a self-destructive cycle of Inquisition which will ultimately transfer each of these gleefully-bloodthirsty persecutors to the interrogation stand is worth a moment of consideration. Behind the theatrical display of Social Justice rage against White Privilege and "solidarity" with the Third World Poor lies nothing more than the same snobbery and cluelessness about the "common people" which led the princess from gated walls to not even know where Conan's Cimmeria was located, only that it was somewhere very far away and populated by barbarians:

> She watched him with timorous fascination . . There was a wolfish hardness about him that marked him as a barbarian. His features, allowing for the strains and stains of battle and his hiding in the marshes, reflected that same untamed wildness, but they were neither evil nor degenerate . . . She [only] knew vaguely that the land he named lay far to the northwest, beyond the farthest boundaries of the different kingdoms of her race.[58]

This reaction is of course far more generous and humanizing than how an ivy league professor in Massachusetts whose entire resume of publications contain references to "The Other" and "Class Struggle" will still react to meeting a working class peasant from flyover Kansas by launching into a lecture about how uncivilized this remote Cimmerian wilderness must be to be filled with its hordes of "barbarians" with bigoted views about people they don't know (an irony our "top intellectual" judging someone from a state

---

[58] Howard, Robert E, *Iron Shadows in the Moon* in *Conan of Cimeria Volume 1* (New York: Ballantine Books, 2003), p. 190.

he has never personally visited will likely still miss.) But we Cimmerian Philosophers lying beyond the frontiers of respectability thrive on this freedom of perspective which would be stifled by the short-lived dead ends which academic fads amount to after the cycle of inflating a speculative bubble for a few years reliably ends with a crash into worthlessness.

    Moreover, Peak Oil is a problem far too serious to be handed over to academic posturers with theories which even *they* don't believe without the financial self-interest of advancing a career on the basis of a rising stock value in, say, Postcolonial or Queer Theory. Even "Classical" Marxist Theory would be utterly useless to solve the crisis of economic inequality stemming from automation, usury, and long distance transport networks, since Marxism's vague notion of "modes of production" misses the fact that any one of these "deepest layers of analysis" is merely a secondary effect of burning through some resource base with a far more fundamental position within the hierarchy. Freudian Psychoanalysis, equally academically fashionable despite being disproven empirically, would be just as inappropriate to solving the crises of political unrest shaking the globe today, since Freud mistakenly thought that the sexual libido was the most foundational drive in a hierarchy of epiphenomena, not realizing that an un-repressed sexual drive is unlikely to accomplish much of anything without a primary energy source to feed the person who has been so graciously "liberated" by identifying some fictitious childhood trauma which normalizes the perversion of *incest* as an insurmountable crime of which we are, supposedly, *all* guilty, whether we admit it or not. The present volume could never have been written with any amount of intellectual honesty or seriousness without discarding such pet theories of the comfortably-tenured "intellectual elite" who enjoy generous six figure salaries in exchange for devoting two hours a week to lecturing on "Radical Theories" while their graduate student assistants grade all of their students' papers, or spending three hours a week sitting in graduate seminar to allow the latest round of sycophantic boot-licking graduate students to compete for "social capital" by outdoing one another in begging the professor to please entertain them with updates about his or her current book project or latest conference presentation. Behind the façade of academia's "radical political engagement with the real world" lies a group of imperial fiddle players who try to hear one another's pretty melodies over the faint sound of flames engulfing the Post-Peak Oil world outside their palaces windows.

### The New Enlightenment Begins

Likewise, Peak Oil Philosophy will differ from the established philosophies of Zizek, Badiou, Heidegger etc. by its requirement to have an overtly anti-academic stance, such that responsible and serious treatment of the problem of Peak Oil is something which could *only* be done in a context that shuns academic fashions and celebrates the utter obscurity out of which the present work is written, some ten thousand miles away from the North American ivory tower locations the author once frequented. The ad hoc community of YouTube viewers that have come to support the author's project of Peak Oil Philosophy in various ways are a burgeoning anti-academic movement of independent thinkers which the author appreciates for making the "New Enlightenment" of enthusiastic collaborators with no regard for academic fads into a reality. As valuable as the old saying that it is very hard to get a man to understand a theory if his salary depends on his not understanding it might be, the author would like to turn this statement around: any person who only understands any theories whatsoever in order to accomplish the teleological task of earning a salary is overwhelmingly unlikely to be interesting company in an intellectual movement anyway. It is difficult to imagine that the "top intellectuals" of our era whose "work" is in many cases literally just a euphemism for finding creative ways to dupe clueless 18 year old kids into selling their souls to six figure student loan debt in exchange for ridiculous courses on Beyoncé and *The Walking Dead* would have anything substantial to contribute to a serious, life or death discussion of the Philosophy of Peak Oil. The clueless academic careerists who emphatically *will not* read the present volume are therefore just so many sour grapes whose presence to the discussion would be as underwhelming as the tuition for their courses is overpriced, even if they did happen to participate.

On the contrary, the writings of preference around which this emerging YouTube community of independent thinkers is forming present a palpable contrast to the latest academic fads. Rather than bow down in an act of coerced denial that the emperor is butt-naked in open view of all and pretend that Intersectional and Transnational "Theory" are anything but outrageously boring pseudo-theories which could be summarized in about 30 seconds of wasted time, this community has developed a noticeable preference for the unacknowledged greatest thinkers of our era: the anti-technology Unabomber Ted Kaczynski and the great Peak Oil green wizard John Michael Greer. Along with Alan Collinge, the lone voice of Truth in a swamp of lies about the student loan usury catastrophe, these make up the three most important thinkers of the present era. In addition, the author extends his gratitude, in friendship, to the viewers of the chadafrican philosophy channel. These four, along with the author's wife Minu, constitute the object of dedication of the present work.

## *The New Leprosy*

A very serious ethical and political problem can also be identified in the diploma mill industry's flawed logic which promotes charging $50,000 per year in tuition as a "good deal" to the poor sucker who gets stuck with the bill for the rest of his or her life; the myth of achieving the American Dream through going deep into student loan debt, as mentioned in in the previous chapter, is all the more dysfunctional for the following reason: what gets left out of the myth that college (or, to cut the bullshit, student loans) will lift the working class out of poverty is the unspeakable fact that with each passing year the number of people who actually get to enjoy the "normal middle class lifestyle" gets smaller and, to an extent few baby boomers will ever admit, older. The systematic loss of opportunity for social mobility for the millennial generation is all the more ironic, given that it is also the most highly-educated generation in the history of the world, a fact which will prove to be one of the great miscalculations of history when enough of the unemployed philosophers of yesteryear find that they can apply their training in Political Philosophy outside the sacred confines of "socially acceptable politically correct liberal thought" (a mere euphemism for upholding middle class privilege and fossil fuel-wasting lifestyles under the laughable banner of "radical social justice politics," as though voting for Hillary Clinton in 2016 amounted to some sort of "revolutionary stance" against the same corporatist and war industrial complex swamp she emerged from like Grendel's mother.) One goal of this book will be to awaken this sleeping giant of disenfranchised youth who are wise enough to know that the "social justice" movement is simply another way for figures already tapped into power, like Hillary Clinton, to try to lobby for even more power on the basis of an obscure pseudo-algorithm to calculate one's "victim index" on the basis of gleefully finding one "intersectional" category of oppression while clinging for dear life to one's membership within all the other markers of privilege. A justifiable sense of alienation has emerged among those outside the senile aristocracy when confronted with the grotesque hypocrisy these figures demonstrate in celebrating this social dance of claiming victimhood in order to gain more access to the spoils of a global, fossil fuel-based empire which required countless real victims to be oppressed at a more than "theoretically intersectional" level.

    The youth of our era, provided they are not forced by the pressure cooker environment of campus conformity into shouting "radical" slogans that only defend the system even more, have come out the losers of an unjust economic arrangement that forced students to finance their own "education" with predatory student loans from which one can *never* escape, just as the price skyrocketed and the real value plummeted for these degrees. For one, the value of these degrees, of course, was harmed by grade inflation, whereby an A+ grade can be obtained for nothing more than the five figure-price of each semester's tuition bill. In addition, with the loudly-trumpeted requirement that "every kid has to get one," the difference between a for profit diploma mill that prints a worthless slip of paper in exchange for a vast sum of cash and a respectable R1 "public ivy" university which does the same thing has dropped down to a mere distinction of marketing. Finally, the cleverly-crafted yet completely false claim that obtaining a college degree would result in a "million dollars of extra income over one's lifetime" contained disturbing echoes of a Ponzi Scheme, as though a bachelor's degree were literally just a lottery ticket which was already guaranteed to win; all one had to do was trade it in for a "million dollar prize" which somehow never did materialize after graduation was over and the student debt collectors started to move in for the kill. Yet the millions of disenfranchised millennials dwelling in their parents' basements in between bartender shifts, a job worked almost exclusively just to provide a little more cash to feed their exploding student loan balances, are a demographic time bomb which is ignored precisely because the "middle class" of our previously-mentioned ordinary lifestyle is not assumed to be the fraction of society which actually get to enjoy its privileges; it is assumed to be a universal set from which only the nefarious "one percent" are excluded, and that is only the case because they are even wealthier and even more privileged

    Yet outside the symbolic gates of this supposedly "universal" set encompassing all the happy motorers in their gas-hungry SUVs stamped with "certified tree hugger" bumper stickers expressing nominal alarm about Climate Change (the physical embodiment of contradiction itself) who have ridden the wave of fossil fuel-based progress into unearned affluence, anyone foolhardy and courageous enough to venture outside these ideological walls will find a vast, sprawling population of untouchables who have long since ceased to even dream of "keeping up with the Joneses," since finding their next meal and spending another night *not* sleeping out in the cold rank a bit higher on the list of priorities. The fact that media pretends these people don't exist and never have existed is a troubling confirmation that Orwell's *1984* statement that "Ocenia is at war with Eastasia and has always been at war with Eastasia" or his *Animal Farm* statement that "Snowball is now in league with Jones and has always been in league with Jones" has officially transitioned from future prophecy to present description.

In addition to the remarkably vast problem of homelessness in every major city, suburb, and even small town in the United States, the natural outcome of artificially supporting real estate bubbles that squeeze both home ownership and rent out of reach of those making less than six figure salaries which are themselves mere redistributions of politically-connected sums of printed money to prop up a handful of predictably-corrupt sectors, a vast leper colony of minimum wage workers toil away at the futile project of cobbling together a living by adding one 20 hour workweek to another from a handful of part-time fast food, retail, and freelance jobs but still find that the harder they work the deeper in debt they end up. The homeless "internal slum dwellers" and the invisible minimum wage workers mopping the floors of retail centres do hold one thing in common: they both cannot be accounted for with the narrow resources of the social justice and "Intersectional Theory" pseudo-systems of political critique. What we need is not another bloated sociological data set, another pseudo-economical number crunching algorithm, or another attempt to beat the dead horse of Marxism to see if this time a real revolution might be waiting behind the curtain; William of Ockham may be pleased to find this many centuries later that a political razor may confirm that "sometimes the simplest option is the right one." Although the liberal "intelligentsia" of our bloated university system have bled the printing presses of an enormous sum of ink to print (largely unread) academic literature on economic inequality, populated by as many mathematically-formalized models and as much empirical data as they think will be required to get them tenure, no amount of linear complication can reach the simple, unspeakable fact that the only word which can properly describe their status is one captured better by *Conan the Cimmerian* than by any highly-paid social "scientist:" *Cimmeria is on the outside, so far on the outside, that the princess only has a vague sense that it's somewhere "out there" beyond the gates of respectability and civilization.*

We Cimmerian philosophers are similarly somewhere "out there," far outside the walls of academic respectability or legitimacy. But as the difficult times projected into the future encroach upon the too-near present, one might find that spending so many years on the inside of a gated ivory tower palace, surrounded by an army of underpaid graduate student and adjunct servants who did all the real work one later got the credit (and the pay-check) for, had made one too soft to endure the harsh gusts of freezing wind which characterize the icy mountain peaks which Nietzsche designated as the habitat of a real philosopher:

> One must be skilled at living on mountains- seeing the wretched ephemeral babble of politics and national self-seeking beneath oneself . . . Rather live in the ice than among modern virtues and other south winds![59]

Or perhaps even *beyond* the ice:

> Let us face ourselves. We are Hyperboreans . . . Beyond the north, beyond the ice, beyond death[60]

At any rate, serious students of Philosophy are almost completely certain to never encounter Peak Oil in the discourses of "leading philosophers" of our era, whether they be legitimate intellectual heavyweights like Slavoj Zizek or careerist straw-men who have sold their soul to the academic equivalent of Satan by agreeing to remake Philosophy into a comical caricature of a pseudo-STEM department, simply with the hope of boosting philosophy's "brand" to gain legitimacy (as well as funding) in the eyes of administrators who, despite the façade of being "politically correct intellectuals bringing education to the masses" are little more than soullessly greedy CEOs intent on bankrupting the youth by packaging six figure student loans in exchange for a flimsy diploma hardly worth its weight in paper. Regarding the official gatekeepers of academic philosophy in the United States, suffice it to say that trying to remake Philosophy in the image of Pure

---

[59] Nietzsche, Friedrich, *The Antichrist* in *The Portable Nietzsche* (New York: Penguin, 1982), p. 569.
[60] Ibid.

Mathematics, Chemistry, Physics, or some other unrelated but "highly prestigious" scientific field is a policy pursued for understandable short-term benefit (not to mention financial self-interest) while utterly destroying what little remaining dignity academic philosophy still held in an era when the "university" itself has become a mere front operation for the predatory student loan industry. At this point, the very term "Academic Philosophy" must be read as something of an inherent contradiction, given that the foxes who now oversee the henhouse are distinguished above all by their aversion to and embarrassment by, ironically enough, Philosophy! One conclusion that Peak Oil will make certain, however, is that such a fad will be remarkably short-lived and, if remembered at all, will merely serve as a testament to the utter madness into which official academic discourse dissolved in its final twilight years.

*The Theoretical Peak Oil Philosophy*

In conclusion of Part I of the present work, it should be noted that the present volume represents the first half of a two-volume work which systematically spells out the meaning of Peak Oil Philosophy according to the traditional philosophical distinction between Theoretical and Practical divisions of Philosophy. Volume I shall examine Peak Oil Philosophy in light of traditionally theoretical problems of Ontology, Epistemology, Truth, Meaning, and the self-reflexive theoretical elucidation of Peak Oil Philosophy's own essence as a unique field of philosophical thought. Volume II shall handle the traditional Practical problems of Ethics, Politics, Religion, and Economics in light of the author's notion of an emerging Cimmerian Philosophy populated by figures explicitly working against the academic fads and bloated institutions whose unstated goal of maximizing the sale of predatory student loans offer no resources to critique Fossil Fuel Modernity, insofar as selling student loans in exchange for ridiculous courses on "how to act like a corporate drone" is itself just a systematic redundancy of the Soma of Fossil Fuels.

Part II
Being

"Open it to four-sixty-seven Kalima- where it says: 'From water does all life begin.'" — Frank Herbert, *Dune*

## Chapter Three:
## Dialectic and Hierarchy:
## Hegelian Negation and Haagian Limitation

The word Ontology suffers from the same problem of ambiguity as its root word. ὄντος, or Being, is every bit as unclear as Ontology, or the Science of Being. One recurring method, therefore, has been to provide a predicate to substitute for this vague subject by supplementing it with a more readily-intelligible metaphor. Deleuze, for example, accomplished this task by arguing for an Ontology of Difference (quite literally, "Being is Difference"); Heidegger did the same by arguing for an Ontology of Dasein ("Being is Disclosure"); Badiou followed with an Ontology of Set Theoretical Mathematics, and Zizek with an Ontology of Incompleteness stemming from the dialectical failure to embody the Notion. In any case, the logic that "difference" or "incompleteness" is more readily-comprehensible than "Being" demonstrated that all along, when one had been talking about "Being" one had really been talking about "difference" or "incompleteness." The author of the present work favours an Ontology of Limitation, such that if one is talking about "Being," one is really talking about "limitation" without knowing it.

One might reasonably object that the formula "Being is Limitation" defeats the purpose of clarification because limitation is perhaps even more mysterious a concept than Being. Even those whom Heidegger critiqued as carrying around the "historically transmitted ontologies" that unwittingly equate Being with Objective Presence still have some understanding of Being, however questionable: but such people will likely have no clear idea at all about what sort of thing limitation is, or even whether it is appropriate to call it a thing.[61]

Limitation remains ambiguous even for those few thinkers who have taken explicit interest in developing their philosophies around it. In an early post from the *Archdruid Report* titled "The

---

[61] Heidegger, Martin. *Being and Time* Trans. Joan Stambaugh (Albany: State University of New York Press, 1996) p. 24.

Shadow of Our Downfall," John Michael Greer noted that David Icke's conspiracy theory about reptilian lizards was nothing more than what Carl Jung called "projecting the shadow." Jung's theory was of course that the "sum total of everything we don't accept about ourselves" would be projected onto a shadow that could serve as the object of a purified and concerted hatred by exteriorizing all the things we despise about ourselves onto some figure who is "out there" and definitely "not me." It is curious, however, to note that the most hated feature about ourselves which the lizards embody is "the reality of limitation."[62] David Icke's theories therefore reached a massive audience through arguing that limitation is not an essential feature of finite human existence; it is just a side effect of the Reptilians' malice: "the Reptilians aren't just to blame for everything wrong with the world, they deliberately created and maintain the illusion of material reality with real, inflexible limits."[63] In other words, limitation would not exist if the Reptilians were not meddling with our minds. Far from affirming an Ontology of Limitation, David Icke implies that the lizards literally generate limitation as the product of their action. Even if we were to accept Icke's thesis, however, the ontological constitution of limitation would still remain hopelessly unclear. Even Icke seems to suggest that the Being of limitation is impossible to describe with the Metaphysics of Objectivity: that is why he never asserts that limitation exists. He merely acknowledges that limitations *seem* to exist as a part of an elaborate illusion devoid of substance.

    Despite his obvious incompatibility with the author's thesis of an Ontology of Limitation, David Icke's reasoning is far more sophisticated than the media acknowledges and is well worthy of consideration. Icke's aversion to limitation stems from the fact that he explicitly argues that consciousness is "infinite" and "limitless" in numerous texts and speeches. Roughly, his theory is that a tiny handful of illuminati insiders control billions of humans on the Earth through preventing us from seeing that we are "infinite consciousness." They do this through tricking us into accepting our

---

[62] John Michael Greer "The Shadow of Our Downfall." In *Archdruid Report* Vol. 1 (Chicago: Founders House, 2017), p. 185.
[63] Ibid., p. 185.

mundane, insignificant personal identities as defined by the system, yet these personal identities are not who we "really are." They are just the "experience," but for Icke the "experience" is not synonymous with consciousness; "the experience" is just a temporary vehicle which infinite consciousness inhabits for a brief period of time but is in no way identical with it. All energy is, in fact, consciousness, insofar as consciousness is an enduring, fundamental element which is misrecognized as a plurality of different entities; he explicitly calls consciousness the "same substance [which is manifested] in different states of being."[64] Likewise, another of Icke's fundamental positions is that things are categorically *not* what they appear to be, since accepting a reductive positivistic empiricism would force one to renounce hopes for limitless consciousness in favour of settling for the disappointing appearance which is immediately given to perception. Illusion therefore holds a central role in Icke's philosophy. He goes as far as to say in *The Robots' Rebellion: The Story of Spiritual Renaissance* that those who fail to heed his message will "go on being mesmerized by this physical world and largely controlled by its illusions and by those misguided forces . . . which seek to turn them into little more than zombies."[65] The ultimate illusion for Icke is, of course, the illusion of limitation, since one can only grasp one's true identity as infinite consciousness if one grasps that a "limitless" consciousness precludes any notion of limitation from truly existing.

    The most interesting question is whether David Icke had committed the error of reification by treating a limitation as a thing by projecting this mysterious notion onto the image of the lizards. Traditionally, "reification" has meant treating abstractions as though they were things and then mistaking the systematic play of abstractions for an insight into how the world of real objects functions.[66] Don Quixote was of course the archetypal example of a

---

[64] See David Icke's interesting text *The Robots' Rebellion: The Story of the Spiritual Renaissance* for a summary of his New Age Cosmology.
[65] Icke, David, *The Robots' Rebellion: The Story of the Spiritual Renaissance* (Gateway).
[66] Greer, John Michael, "Round in Circles: A Review of David C. Korten's *The*

man incapable of distinguishing between abstractions and things, as he expected his own battle with windmills, barbers, and prison guards to unfold the same way that the battle between pure abstractions like "Good" and "Evil" had done in his chivalric books.[67]

The question of whether limitation is an abstraction is further complicated by the fact that there is not only one class of abstractions which all fit under some universal genus; one cannot even determine the class of abstractions through the negative criteria of not being physical objects because each transcendental layer of meaning presents a different set of abstractions. Good and Evil are mythological abstractions capable of presentation only within the layer of Mythology. Positive and negative are gnostic abstractions capable of presentation only at the layer of System. Useful and useless are ergonic (from ἔργον, the Greek word for "work") abstractions capable of presentation only at the layer of Sense Objectivity. Progress (of an ascending ray), completion (of a circle), reciprocity (of a level plane), and decline (of a bell curve) are memological abstractions capable of presentation only at the level of Memology. Presence and absence are somatic abstractions capable of proper presentation only at the level of the Soma. Limitation, however, is not unique to any of these specific classes of abstraction. Limitation is not a mythological personality embodying virtue or vice; nor is limitation a systematic value situated in determinate rank relative to other values; nor is limitation conducive to the continued flow of ἔργον (work) or an inhibition which would halt it from continuing; nor is limitation a single one of the four deep memes, such that the other three would have no relation to limitation; nor is limitation unique to any one of the somatic bodies (big game, agrarian grain, fossil fuels, salvage) such that the other three would be free from it.

Even across five transcendental registers of meaning, it is impossible to present limitation as such in any one of them. This is not evidence that limitation "doesn't exist" (or more specifically, that limitation has no Being.) Rather, Being itself cannot be

---

*Great Turning* in *The Archdruid Report* Vol. 1 (Chicago: Founders House, 2017), p. 163.
[67] Cervantes, Miguel, *Don Quixote* (New York: Penguin, 2001), p. 165.

understood outside of limitation. Martin Heidegger's need to reawaken the question of Ontology stemmed from a similar inability to talk about Dasein within the intellectual framework of the ontic realm of present objects or even within one of Husserl's established regions of Material Ontology.[68] Heidegger's famous insight that "Being is not a being" must be reapplied to limitation: limitation is not a being, for if it were it could be situated within one of the five registers. Limitation itself is not even a somatic body. Limitation in itself is not *a being*, for it is Being. David Icke's error in treating limitation as specific beings (the lizards) is therefore far more dangerous than one might realize just from the superficial view of "reification of abstraction."

Limitation is arguably the single most controversial concept in our era. This is best evidenced by the sheer rarity with which it is discussed at all, except in cases where it is openly repudiated. Serious investigations of the concept of limitation that do not take the negative path of dismissing it therefore merit our attention before proceeding to a more detailed analysis of the Ontology of Limitation. Notably, it has been over 50 years since Frank Herbert's classic 1965 Science Fiction novel *Dune*, one of the most important meditations on limits to occur in the past century. In *Dune* the desert planet Arrakis is a place where water is so precious that one would make a fatal error by treating it as a being interpretable through the Metaphysics of Objectivity. To see water on Arrakis as an object suitable for analysis in terms of positive predicates such as colour, clarity, temperature, and taste would be to gravely misunderstand that water is not one object among many others on Arrakis. Water is the limit to life. Neglecting the latter in favour of the former perspective will guarantee nothing except an early death by thirst:

> There were water riots when it was learned how many people the Duke was adding to the population . . . There is only so much water to support human life here . . . The

---

[68] Heidegger, Martin, *Being and Time* (Albany: State University of New York Press, 1996), p. 9.

people know if more come to drink a limited amount of water, the price goes up and the very poor die.[69]

One must be aware of the limits of water on Arrakis; but of what does this awareness consist? Could one be aware of a limitation the way one is aware of a blacksmith hammer in one's hands, or the warmth of the fire in a wood-burning stove on a cold winter night, or the bitter taste of black coffee? Is a limitation accessible to the senses' perceptions of things in the world? Is limitation somewhere buried within the contents mined from what Husserl called the "hyletic data" (from ὕλη, the Ancient Greek word for "matter," or more precisely from Aristotle's adoption of the word for "wood" for that purpose) and what Bertrand Russell called sense data?[70] Under this view, limitation would have to have a colour, a taste, a tactile character, or a smell to fit within the mixture of raw sensations which are distinct even from the objects which they are later interpreted to be through either Phenomenological (Husserl) or logical (Russell) constructs.

In *Dune*, water's limitation requires a methodology that is decidedly different from that of empiricist scientific investigation, but it is a perfectly justifiable concept to contemplate nonetheless. In fact, being able to grasp the importance of limitation represents one of the highest acts of a thinking subject. *Dune* is a novel which really centres on the project of salvaging thinking subjects against the onslaught of machines that would seek to obviate the very need for thinking. The novel opens with a discussion of the dangers of outsourcing thinking to machines which had admittedly overtaken humans in terms of computing power:

> Once men turned their thinking over to machines in the hope that this would set them free. But that only permitted other men with machines to enslave them.[71]

---

[69] Herbert, Frank, *Dune* (New York: Ace Books, 1990), p. 63.
[70] Bertrand Russell *The Problems of Philosophy* p. 26 and Edmund Husserl *Ideas* p. 283.
[71] Herbert, Frank, *Dune* (New York: Ace Books, 1990), p. 11.

The rise of thinking machines "made in the likeness of a man's mind" naturally led to an attempt to salvage human thought while it was still possible, but it is interesting to note that this was not to be accomplished through trying to outcompete machines in narrowly-defined tasks like number crunching speed and raw data storage volume, areas at which the machines had already well surpassed humans.

The novel's protagonist Paul is one such person selected to develop his mind through training to become a mentat. "Mentat" is a term coined from the Latin word for mind ("mens") by Herbert to describe a person who has been selected to salvage human thinking amidst the rapid development of hostile machines; the mentat would do so by undergoing a rigorous set of training exercises to develop the mind itself in the absence of help from machines or other artificial stilts. The naïve view might assume that the mentats did so by seeking to outcompete machines at their specializations, such as raw processing speed or data storage potential: however, the mentats largely distinguished themselves from machines by developing the features which any machine, no matter how complicated or powerful, lacked: awareness. Machines can process data; but they cannot be aware. The mentats therefore devote their energies to developing this amazing ability which is so often taken for granted or squandered by those who are all too eager to trade it in for a cheap artificial intelligence surrogate. The mentats even manage to expand awareness from the mundane level of "seeing sense contents" to more mysterious levels of consciousness, such as seeing motives, seeing changes, and hearing falsehood:

> Mentat training was supposed to give a man the power to see motives.[72]
>
> Paul said[,] 'The spice changes anyone who gets this much of it, but . . . I could bring the change to consciousness. I don't get to leave it in the unconscious where its disturbance can be blanked out. I can *see* it.[73]

---

[72] Ibid., p. 208.
[73] Ibid., p. 196.

Paul heard the falsehood in their voices, felt the menace that had brought Halleck instinctively into guarding position.[74]

Naïve technophiles who gamble that consciousness, not only for themselves but for whole of humanity, is so cheap as to be recklessly traded in for a transhumanist migration into machines are fooling themselves if they think that being uploaded into a fossil fuel-burning machine will not mean completely surrendering their (admittedly undeveloped) mentatic abilities; the common word for such a loss, one should be reminded, used to be *death,* yet it is somehow being portrayed as "eternal life." Even if this change does somehow occur, the only thing they will find on the inside of a machine is the sheer darkness in which no consciousness is possible.

In addition to seeing motives, seeing changes, and hearing falsehood, the mentats' ultimate test for awareness is the ability to achieve awareness of limits. One of the most important parts of Paul's training as a mentat involved receiving a copy of the *Orange Catholic Bible,* a text that would be passed down over generations as part of a rite of initiation. When he is first given a glimpse into a physical copy of the book, he remarks that it looks quite old, like it was "made before filmbooks."[75] Interestingly, when he reads aloud from the book, he does not find the kind of information so prized by the Religion of Progress in our era: the book is not filled with the latest scientific research or the latest industrial trends, both of which quickly lose their value and devolve to utter worthlessness when no longer able to claim the title of being "current." The logic behind the *Orange Catholic Bible* is completely opposite: not only is there a total disregard for recent trends, the content of the book itself is not scientific research on the objectively accessible realm of sense contents. It is instead filled with cryptic, nearly mystical, wisdom on the concept of limitation: examples include the sayings "From water does all life begin" and

---

[74] Ibid., p. 125.
[75] Ibid., p. 40.

Think of the fact that a deaf person cannot hear. Then, what deafness may we not all possess? What senses do we lack that we cannot see and cannot hear another world all around us?[76]

The highest thinker is the one able to transcend mythology, system, objects, memes, and even the Soma itself to contemplate the notion of limitation, precisely insofar as limitation itself is not to be found in any of these. Yet the highest achievement of the mentat is to somehow gain awareness of limitation. One could argue that such an act would mean gaining awareness of Being rather than of beings.

Another classical meditation on limits occurred in Michel Foucault's greatest work *The Archaeology of Knowledge*. This was his only fully methodological work that provided an explicit account of his general philosophy which was only indirectly deducible from his earlier works on specific topics such as madness, the clinic, and the contingency of the Human Sciences. These previous works were in a certain sense historical texts. *Madness and Civilization*, for example, presented something of a history of madness but actively rejected the standard subjectivist metaphors by which history was usually conducted. Foucault did not present a "biography of madness," in which madness would be portrayed as one single thing with an intrinsic nature that remained unchanged over the millennia; under this view, the rise of Modern Psychiatry would be the "happy moment" when scientists finally recognized madness for what it had intrinsically been all along and finally set upon treating it properly.[77] Foucault demonstrated instead that it was improper to speak of a biography of madness in which one single object endured over the centuries, merely awaiting the moment that it would be correctly diagnosed by the modern psychiatrist: madness was instead many different things at many different times. This of course required a theoretical explanation for why models of history that privileged subjective metaphors had to

---

[76] Ibid.
[77] Foucault, Michel, *Madness and Civilization* (New York: Vintage House, 1965), p. 241.

be rejected. The idea of historical periods (such as the 18th Century) misapplied the coherence and endurance of a (presumed) subject to the realm of history. Yet Foucault argued that it was more appropriate to speak of rupture and discontinuity than integration and continuity.[78]

Shifting the emphasis to ruptures and discontinuities posed a philosophical challenge, though, because these were terms that were not interpretable with the resources of a Metaphysics of Objectivity, or even a Metaphysics of Subjectivity, as Foucault was fond of situating himself in opposition to Phenomenological notions of subjective constitution.[79] Much of Foucault's argument in *The Archaeology of Knowledge* therefore centred on an interest in limits. He noted that limits are difficult to address with the currently-established philosophical theories because limits are neither interior nor exterior to the field of which they are the limitation. The interior fallacy would mistake a limit as lying in the "connection among words" while the exterior fallacy would mistake a limit as a transcendent "form imposing influence" upon the field.[80]

The following illustration will help clarify. Given a set of elements {a, b, c, d, e}, it would be difficult to designate what the limit of this series is without falling into the interior or exterior fallacies. The interior fallacy would lead one to misrecognize one of the specific elements within the set to be the limit of the whole set: for example, one might naively assume that because 'a' and 'e' are first and last items in the list (that is, they are the delimiters), they are the limits. Yet designating an element as the limit will launch one onto the hamster wheel of infinite recursion: if 'a' is the limit of the series, then what is the limit of 'a?' If one were forced to add supplementary elements to act as the limits of the delimiters, one would simply generate a larger series: {**z**, a, b, c, d, e, **f**}. One

---

[78] Foucault, Michel, *The Archaeology of Knowledge* (New York: Vintage Books, 2010), p. 4.
[79] Foucault's opposition to Husserlian Phenomenology is most explicitly visible in his interviews collected in *Power Knowledge: Selected Interviews and Writings 1972-1977* (New York: Pantheon, 1980).
[80] Ibid., p. 46.

would then have to add further supplements to provide the limits of the limits of the limits: {**y**, z, a, b, c, d, e, f, **g**}.

The exterior fallacy would make the same error but change the location of concern from an element within the set to an element outside the set. One might assume that the limit to the set {a, b, c, d, e} was some transcendent X which lay outside the set and exercised its influence upon each of the elements from one remove away: for example, X → {a, b, c, d, e}. Nietzsche's resistance to dualisms of all kinds fit with this rejection of any transcendent X beyond the set of appearances, such as the Christian heaven, the Kantian Thing in Itself, and the Platonic World of Ideas. Foucault was similarly sceptical of dualisms but qualified his criticism with the philosophical insight that in these cases, one had still failed to grasp limitation as such: the transcendent X was not a limit to the set- it was just another super-element transposed to the outside of the series but bearing no ontological difference from any of the minor elements contained on the inside. Grasping limitation as such would require abandoning any of the presuppositions indigenous to the elements of the set.

Jordan Peterson was arguably the last great thinker to write seriously on the topic of limitation. Interestingly, he also dabbled with an Ontology of Limitation of sorts in his recent book *12 Rules for Life*, though as a self-help book written for a general audience by a psychologist rather than philosopher, many of his insights on the topic are quite vague. At one point in Rule 12, he speculates that "Being of any reasonable sort appears to require limitation."[81] Interestingly, Peterson uses the Superman comic book franchise to explain this strange claim. The original Superman had admittedly impressive abilities like being able to lift cars and run as fast as a train, but these abilities were supplemented over time by more and more superhuman ones: in successive issues, he was able to lift planets and survive nuclear blasts. Eventually, Superman was effectively limitless, capable of surviving any attack and capable of performing any feat in response. But a Superman who did not suffer in some way from limitation became boring and the substance of

---

[81] Peterson, Jordan, *12 Rules for Life* (New Delhi: Allen Lane, 2018), p. 345.

Kryptonite had to be invented to consciously introduce limitation into his world. In addition to humanizing him, Kryptonite also solved a crucial narratological problem: no limitation means no story, as limitation is the only thing that launches a narrative into effect as a struggle against a limitation, even one as artificially introduced into the universe as Kryptonite. Peterson himself speculates:

> Perhaps this is because Being requires Becoming, as well as mere static existence- and to become is to become something more, or at least something different. That is only possible for something limited.[82]

Existence is therefore a striving towards becoming something more; if a being were complete, there would be no need for this striving because this "more" would vanish. The mystery is what ontological status this "more" holds. Is it just another object which could ideally be concatenated onto the subject to form a composite super-subject as its result? Or is this "more" just a subjective illusion which fulfils the practical psychological need of having some goal, however contrived, to avoid insanity? Or is the "more" precisely the limitation which would seem to preclude the subject from obtaining it?

An examination of Kryptonite might help resolve these questions. Kryptonite is something of a condensation of limitation into object form, like "limitation purified" into a single, coherent essence. David Icke's lizards also condense limitation into a single essence, but that is only for the purpose of promising that someday limitation can be overcome through destroying the lizards. In Superman's universe, however, the opposite is the case: Kryptonite is reintroduced back into the universe precisely because removing limitation deprived Superman of his existential subjectivity and degraded him to the status of a lifeless puppet, something for which even inauthenticity had been lost as an option![83] Yet Kryptonite's

---

[82] Ibid., p. 345.
[83] See Martin Heidegger's *Being and Time* section II.1 for a discussion on existentialist inauthenticity and authenticity.

objective form is merely a symbolic expression for the notion of limitation; in itself, limitation has none of the minimal categorical features of an object. One cannot understand the ontological problem of limitation through the ontic resources of a green rock any more than one could understand Dasein through some de-worlded object present at hand.

Although Limitation is not an Object, it wold be wrong to dismiss Kryptonite out of hand as a useless metaphor for the "ineffable mystical essence" of limitation. On the contrary, Kryptonite is remarkably useful for launching a detailed analysis of the Ontology of Limitation for the following reason: one could argue that Kryptonite is Superman's "determinate limitation." Rather than simply say that "Superman has limits" in an abstract sense without further qualification, Kryptonite provides a determinate content: Superman's limitation *is* Kryptonite.

The paradox, of course, is that limitation is not an object yet can somehow still be determinate. The author acknowledges his own indebtedness to Hegel for providing a similar insight about determinate negation, though the present work is emphatically not to be read as a work of dialectical philosophy. Hegel's Philosophy is best understood as a lengthy meditation on Imminent Critique. Hegel rejected correspondence theories of truth which defined truth as the agreement between mind and world (Ancient Greek Philosophy), mind of man and mind of God (Medieval Philosophy), or proposition and fact (Modern Analytic Philosophy.) For Hegel, there was no need for an agreement between the Notion and some transcendent entity because the Notion itself had already failed to live up to its own criteria. The problem is not so much that the Notion fails to depict some object on the outside correctly: the problem is that the Notion has failed be itself. In ordinary discourse, we express a similar idea of truth when we ask whether something is true gold or fool's gold: there is no need to go beyond the rock to examine whether it has succeeded in being what it was supposed to be.

Each of the phases of Hegel's *Phenomenology of Spirit* repeats this failure to embody the Notion despite generating finer and finer grades of sophistication. The first section, Consciousness, for example, fails to achieve consciousness of the object. Sense Certainty opens with the hope for absolute certainty based on the immediacy of the senses but finds that restriction to what is "here" and "now" fails both to be immediate (since here and now are actually Universals in disguise) and to be certain (since with the passage of time, "here" is a tree at one time but is a house at another and "now" is day at one time and night at another.)[84] Sense Certainty has therefore always already failed to escape negation, even at the moment it explicitly removed the pathways to negation by focusing only on what is "here" and "now." The negation of Sense Certainty, in which Sense Certainty is revealed to be *not* absolute certainty based on the senses, leads the Notion on an odyssey of development into phases of scientific, historical, cultural, religious, and ethical episodes that would have been unimaginable with the resources available simply from the naïve positive glimpse into the Notion of "Consciousness" that began the work.

      Negation, like limitation, is of course not an object. Even those who conceive of negation as simply the opposite of Being or the lack of Being remain stuck within the narrow definition of negation which Hegel called abstract negation: this is a simple "no" without further qualification. The negation operator in Formal Logic, the tilde or ~ symbol, is only capable of symbolizing abstract negation: the only purpose of negation in such a system is to flip the truth value of its operand from true to false or from false to true. The logical expression (~True) would yield False as its result, just as the logical expression (~False) would yield True but in itself, the negation operator ~ can do nothing because it is merely a higher order operation upon operands. Under this view, the operator is dependent upon its operands because they embody the full, independent Being which negation lacks. Logicist thinkers like Frege and Russell did not find this to be an inadequate definition of negation, for only abstract negation was sufficiently logical to merit inclusion in their systems. Yet Hegel argued that the abstract negation of a simple "no" was to be contrasted from the determinate

---

[84] Hegel, G. W. F. *Phenomenology of Spirit*. (Oxford: Oxford University Press, 1977), pp.60-62.

negation or negation with a content. The following quote from Hegel's Introduction to the *Science of Logic* explicates this distinction:

> [W]hat is self-contradictory does not resolve itself into a nullity, into abstract nothingness, but essentially only into the negation of its particular content, in other words, that such a negation is not all and every negation but the negation of a specific subject matter which resolves itself, and consequently is a [determinate] negation and therefore the result essentially contains that from which it results ...[85]

Hegel argued that abstract negation is to be distinguished from determinate negation in that determinate negation is the negation of negation which does not merely reduce its subject to the destruction of nothingness but rather "contains it, but also something more, and is the unity of itself and its opposite." Determinate negation allows a "system of Notions" to emerge through enabling the Notion to imminently develop its content into a gallery of phases which do not merely actualize pre-given potentialities or reproduce forms already determined beforehand but rather generate unexpected results precisely from *within* the Notion's own failure to embody its own meaning completely.[86]

What is most strange about Hegel's view on negation is that it is actually incorrect to say that each phase of dialectic *never* manages to achieve the content of what it is supposed to be. In Hegel's *Philosophy of Mind*, the final volume of the Encyclopaedia, it is not true to say that Art never succeeds in becoming Art. The paradox is that once it does, it is no longer art: it is Religion. Religion, in turn, eventually does overcome the failure to be Religion, but at that point it is no longer Religion: it is Philosophy.[87]

---

[85] Hegel, G. W. F. *The Science of Logic* (Kindle Edition)
[86] Zizek emphasizes that Hegelian Dialectic cannot be understood through the Aristotelian schema of a pre-given potentiality that is actualized by motion in his 900 page book on Hegel, *Less Than Nothing: Hegel and the Shadow of Dialectical Materialism* (Verso: London, 2012).
[87] Hegel, G. W. F. *Philosophy of Mind* (Oxford: Clarendon Press, 1894), pp.342-

This only occurred, in turn, because of the imminent negation of its own content. Hegel explains this role of a negation of negation in the Introduction to the *Science of Logic* as follows:

> Because the result, the negation, is a [determinate] negation, it has content. It is a fresh Notion, but higher and richer than its predecessor, for it is richer by the negation or opposite of the latter, therefore contains it, but also something more, and is the unity of itself and its opposite. It is in this way that the system of Notions as such has to be formed.[88]

The system of Notions is therefore generated through the determinate negation which "has content" despite being negation. Yet this should not be read as some mystical overcoming whereby an alienated content is recovered through correcting the optical illusion that it was on the outside in the first place, as Zizek is fond of repeating in his many analyses of Hegel.[89] Determinate Negation does not prove that all along there really had been an identity free of negation; instead, it demonstrates that one can only achieve Art through departing from the realm of Art altogether. Each of the major phases of *Phenomenology of Spirit* demonstrate this logic: Consciousness struggles through Sense Certainty of the immediate, Perception of a thing, and Understanding of the force and its laws to try to really achieve Consciousness; but Consciousness is only really achieved in the next section of Self-Consciousness. The "Truth of Self Certainty" section which introduces Self-Consciousness into the book presents consciousness as unproblematically given, despite being something which the previous sections had strived after so laboriously and so inconclusively. By this time, consciousness is no longer the merely logical identity of I=I; the I has instead become an interior stirring passion which the I can really feel itself. Consciousness has finally arrived with the rise of Life within the *Phenomenology of Spirit*, a

---

367.
[88] Hegel, G. W. F., *The Science of Logic* (Kindle Edition)
[89] Zizek, Slavoj, *The Parallax View* (Cambridge: MIT Press, 2009), p. 46.

concept unknown before even in the lengthy meditation on the scientific Force of Modern Physics:

> It is the simple genus which, in the movement of Life itself, does not exist for itself qua this simple determination; on the contrary, in this result, Life points to something other than itself, viz. to consciousness, for which Life exists as this unity, or as genus.[90]

Self-Consciousness achieves consciousness precisely through departing from the realm of Consciousness, just as Life achieves Force precisely through departing from out of the realm of Understanding.

The problem, of course, would be achieving Self-Consciousness within its own section. This section would be followed by the famous Slave Master dialectic, in which Self-Consciousness would be proven to depend upon the bizarre requirements of recognition and desire for the desire of the Other (resources that would have been absolutely unthinkable in the previous Consciousness sections which never depended upon positing a second Consciousness, let alone gaining recognition from it.) The aftermath of the Slave Master Dialectic would prove even more unsatisfactory for embodying the Notion. The Unhappy Consciousness section that concludes Self-Consciousness splits Self-Consciousness into the Medieval sinner and the transcendent God, with ascetic mortification of the flesh and renunciation of earthly desires making up the sinner's struggle to overcome this dualism. He follows up by surrendering his will to the mediation of the priest but finds that the priest embodies a bizarre position: the priest is a particular individual man who speaks for the universal will of God:

> [The sinner] lets the mediating minister express this certainty . . . But in this object, in which it finds that its own action and being, as being that of this particular

---

[90] Hegel, G. W. F., *Phenomenology of Spirit* (Oxford: Oxford University Press, 1977), pp.108-9.

consciousness, are being and action in themselves, there has arisen for consciousness the idea of Reason, of the certainty that, in its particular individuality, it has being absolutely in itself, or is all reality.[91]

The priest, therefore, ends the section by paving the way for an individual man whose consciousness overlaps with the universal realm of eternal truths. While the priest's intellect merely transmits the arbitrary claims to universality stemming from the decrees of the Roman Church, the figure of Reason emerges to instead present an individual person whose mind overlaps with the universal realm of mathematical, logical, and scientific truths. The Cartesian cogito that opens up the following Reason section therefore finally achieves self-consciousness by finding the truth within its own mind as a truth accessible within the interior opening of consciousness to itself. Self-Consciousness, therefore, is only achieved after departing from Self-Consciousness to Reason.

    This movement would repeat for the remaining sections of the *Phenomenology*: Spirit achieves Reason through transcending it, just as Religion achieves Spirit by transcending it, and Absolute Knowing achieves Religion by overcoming the final stage of Picture Thinking of the Absolute. In *For They Know Not What They Do*, Zizek argues that this is evidence supporting an interpretation of Hegel as the ultimate anti-Platonist philosopher: whereas for Plato Notional Thinking is the pathway to Truth because the notions really exist in the World of Ideas, for Hegel the Notion is something of a fraud that doesn't really exist, for the moment it embodies the Notion it is lost through the dialectical dissolution that changes the Notion itself.[92] Zizek mentioned this of course to argue for an interpretation of Hegel as the forerunner of an Ontology of Incompleteness which defined Zizek's own sprawling body of work.

    Regardless of how far exactly Zizek and Hegel actually agree, it is clear that Hegel did not consider the Notion to be just a

---

[91] Hegel, G. W. F., *Phenomenology of Spirit* (Oxford: Oxford University Press, 1977), p. 138.
[92] Zizke, Slavoj, *For They Know Not What They Do* (London: Verso, 2008).

linguistic construct useful only for secondarily representing a Being which lay beyond it: "The absolute truth of being is the known Notion and the Notion as such is the truth of being."[93] The question of Fundamental Ontology is therefore accessible only in terms of the Notion, yet the Notion can itself only be understood through negation. Hegel's Ontology is therefore one which does not posit Negation as a secondary feature lying outside Being, or as a privation which lacks Being altogether: Being can only be understood through negation.

The author is not a Hegelian thinker and the present work is not a piece of dialectical philosophy. In fact, the author's disagreements with Hegel are among the most vital resources for grasping the unique vision of the present work. However, the author does find Hegel's general insight that a particular Notion can only achieve its content through departing from its territory to be a useful means for speaking about the Ontology of Limitation. As mentioned earlier, limitation is similar to negation in that limitation is not an object yet limitation can somehow be determinate. Kryptonite is Superman's limitation yet it is neither one positive object among all the other mundane things in Superman's world nor is it simply the privation of Being or a pure abstract nothingness. A determinate limitation has a content but its content is meaningful in relation to the field which is limited by it. Clarification for this admittedly cryptic claim will require revisiting Haag's hierarchy of meanings.

In Parts I and II of the present text, we concerned ourselves with documenting the five transcendental registers of meaning and the unique requirements of manifestation which each embodies. Content cannot be arbitrarily moved from one register to another without sacrificing its integrity as the particular kind of content one hoped to transfer. One cannot, for example, move a systematic value into the register of objectivity without departing from the layer of system altogether, in which case one would no longer be dealing with a value. The five layers are related to one another by far more than just this one negative feature of incommensurability, however. In fact, the author shall argue that what Hegel envisioned

---

[93] Hegel, G. W. F., *The Science of Logic* (Kindle Edition)

in dialectic can be rephrased in terms of transcendental registers of meaning and what Hegel envisioned in negation can be rethought in terms of limitation. This shift from negation to limitation will provide the chief reason for why Peak Oil Philosophy cannot be reduced to any dialectical theory, idealist or materialist.

    Paradoxically, each deeper layer accomplishes what the layer above it seeks to express precisely by abandoning the transcendental requirements unique to that layer. For example, mythology is the default horizon of meaning but it can never overcome the problem of ambiguity. Any mythic event is open to a plurality of interpretations, none of which can ever conclusively establish itself to be the sole correct one. It is not at all clear, for example, whether Barabbas really is or is not a Christian by the end of Lagerkvist's novel *Barabbas* since he demonstrated sufficient willpower to die for identifying himself as a Christian but demonstrated a complete misunderstanding of the meaning of Christianity by joining in Nero's burning of Rome and attributing it to Christianity's "true message." Nor could it ever be conclusively settled whether Macbeth really is destined by fate to become king or whether he misinterpreted the witches' intentionally-deceitful prediction as a self-fulfilling prophecy that unnecessarily led to both the king's and his own death.

    Mythological events are also vague because they embody universal concerns such as good and evil. But these ultimate concerns are inconclusively present in the characters; any believable character will be an indeterminate mixture of both. Characters are decidedly not abstract elements restricted to one value (Good) or the other (Evil.) It is not at all clear, for example, whether Achilles or Hector is any more good or any more evil than the other, as the reader of the *Iliad* will waver among feelings of pity, admiration, horror, and disapproval with regard to both men's actions as warriors fighting for honour, family, and people.

    This limitation of ambiguity drives the myths to strive for clarity and exactness in the form of a "perfect myth" but, strangely, the "perfect myth" can only be achieved by departing from the mythic horizon altogether. Systematic value is in a certain sense precisely what myth strived to be. Value overcomes narratological ambiguity insofar as systematic values such as "12" are exact and specific; 12 is definitively *one* number and not another such as 11 or 13 just as the logical operator & is definitively a conjunction operation and not a disjunction operator (V) or a hypothetical operator (→). Peano counted on being able to axiomatize Arithmetic on the promise that designating only one successor for each number would be sufficient grounds to generate the Whole Number Series on logical grounds alone. The successor of the successor of zero (ss0) is 2 because each number has only one successor: the successor of 2 cannot be both 3 and 4. It can be only be one of them. Even as early as Plato, the difference between numbers and ambiguous linguistic messages was attributed in the *Cratylus* to the inability to modify a number without changing its meaning altogether:

> Cratylus: [T]he case of language . . . is very different. For when by the help of grammar we assign the letters ['A'] or ['B'] or any other letter to a certain name, then, if we add or subtract or misplace a letter, the name which is written is not only written wrongly but not written at all and in any of these cases becomes other than a name . . .
>
> Socrates: I believe that what you say may be true about numbers, which must be just as they are, or not be at all. For example, the number ten at once becomes other than ten if a unit be added or subtracted, and so of any number, but this does not apply to that which is qualitative or anything which is represented under an image.[94]

Poetical statements uttered from the transcendental standpoint of a mythological event differ from mathematical symbols written out in the gnostic register of systematicity because mythological statements can suffer drastic swings in modification without losing meaning but numbers cannot be written with even a single modification without ceasing to be the number they are. One can

---

[94] Plato, *Cratylus*, in *Collected Dialogues* (Princeton: Princeton University Press, 1990), p. 466.

recount the Myth of Lord Brahma's creation of the first woman, in which he was aroused by his own creation, either as the story of a woman who fled from Lord Brahma in the form of a cow, then a doe, then a mare or one can tell the myth as a story of how the woman fled behind, to the left, and then to the right of Lord Brahama and led him to create three extra faces in the process. In both cases, we have the myth of Lord Brahma creating femininity in order to correct his initial mistake of only creating the masculine half of Creation and then falling in love with this first woman who flees from him and leads, ironically, to more creation in the process. In a certain sense, they are both the same myth. But one cannot write the number 10 with any modification without losing the number 10: the number 100 is not 10, nor is the number 1, although both of these add or subtract only a single numerical literal to the original expression. This guarantee for clarity through uniqueness is the basis for systems' overcoming the ambiguity of Mythology. In a sense therefore, Mythology only becomes what it strove to be by becoming System, just as in Hegel's *Phenomenology of Spirit* Self-Consciousness only becomes Self-Consciousness by becoming Reason.

     Yet achieving systematicity over mythology generates its own crisis of limitation which drives the system to strive for perfection as well. It is true that the particular values of a system are each clear (the number 21 is not the number 22, for example) but the systems' ability to express meaning at the macro level remains inconclusive. As was already mentioned, the Google Algorithm uses 2 Billion lines of instruction but expresses only unclearly the ideology of technological intermediation and automation of human capabilities out of existence. The US Tax Code is some 73,954 pages of symbolic complication which only the most entrenched insiders are competent to utilize for its true teleological purposes, which is to allow the wealthy to abuse a convoluted system to pay as small a share of taxes as possible while shifting the burden onto the ordinary citizen who lacks armies of accountants and lawyers with insider knowledge of an intentionally obfuscated tax code. The Ancient Babylonian Code of Hammurabi lists some 282 laws, a relatively large number to reflect an advanced civilization and major imperial power. This is of course dwarfed by the United States' legal code which is so vast that no one is exactly sure how many different possible crimes it forbids. At the very least, we can be sure that it has grown from an estimated 3,000 crimes in 1982 to an estimated 4,450 in 2008. Yet this system's growth in size did not lead to greater clarity for the system as a whole, let alone to a more just society (its supposed purpose.) On the contrary, it is more unclear now than ever just how many ways one might unwittingly break the law on a single day. Jim Rickards' 2016 book *Road to Ruin* documented the shocking ease with which one can find oneself guilty of a "crime" in the contemporary United States of America. He estimated that the legal code had become so convoluted that the average citizen commits some three felonies per day:

> By the 1970s, federal intrusion into land use, employment practices, health care, banking, investment, education, transportation, mining, manufacturing, energy and other spheres was ubiquitous. Every civil regulatory scheme had a complementary criminal enforcement club behind it. Once core criminal laws were amplified with conspiracy, reporting, and false statement statutes, the web was complete. [The] estimate of three felonies a day is no exaggeration.[95]

Rickards goes on to note that it is not only the legal code that has exploded in recent decades but the frequency of extreme interventions by law enforcement as well:

> Between 1980 and 2001, the number of paramilitary style police raids annually in the United States increased from approximately 3,000 to 45,000.[96]

Tens of thousands of SWAT raids are a troubling sign but this number is still absolutely dwarfed by the total number of arrests, as

---

[95] Rickards, Jim, *The Road to Ruin: The Global Elites' Secret Plan for the Next Financial Crisis* (Hudson: Penguin, 2016).
[96] Ibid.

some 70 million Americans have a criminal background of some kind. The legal code of course states unclearly in thousands of crimes and millions of arrests what is actually a very simple essence: a complicated legal code benefits the rich and disadvantages the poor insofar as a complex legal system is intrinsically unjust. Someone sufficiently wealthy to employ an army of lawyers can find a loophole to get out of quite literally any crime, while a poor person who cannot afford even one lawyer will find himself liable to be imprisoned for quite literally any crime. It would be too simplistic to call this ideology, for ideology implies a type of false consciousness of a vague truth hidden behind the surface. This is not some illusory ideology: it is rather just the essence of the legal system spelled out clearly in one image and (intentionally) unclearly in millions of systematic branches.

The strangest feature of the Gnostic register of Systems is that the systems expand in order to overcome inconclusiveness but only become more inconclusive in the process. This is a confusion which challenges the very logic of systems. One would assume that if one symbol were clear, then a million symbols would be a million times clearer. The systems themselves have no resources to explain why this is not the case, for the explanation can only lie in the systems' limitation by that which is *not* systematic.

Even though each particular mathematical symbol within the tax code is clear on its own (that is, a specific number or operator within the code is unambiguous on an individual level) and each particular symbol within the legal code is clear on its own (five years in prison for one crime etc.) the system as a whole remains inconclusive, no matter how linearly complicated or quantitatively vast it becomes. In fact, greater and greater levels of internal complication are the systems' natural response to strive to overcome the type of ambiguity which is generated at the level of the system as a whole despite overcoming it at the level of individual symbols within the system. The system strives to overcome limitation in just the same way that mythology had striven to do so.

Just as the systematic value was the determinate limitation to Mythology, the sense object is the determinate limitation to the System. A sense object is exactly what a systematic value strives to become: systems tend to explode in size and complication yet only ever imperfectly express within the medium of millions of abstract values what can be clearly expressed with only one single sense object. The Google Algorithm states less clearly in two billion lines of abstract symbolic value what a single machine can express in the form of a sense object. Yet the sense object of a machine expresses the same message as the deep meme of progress; the machine states the concept of progress less clearly in the objective form of a "deal with the devil" to burn a finite amount of fossil fuels in order to get an infinite return of perpetual progress.

A lawyers' bill charging prohibitively high fees is, contrary to expectation, not a systematic value located in the gnostic register. It is a counter sense object which manifests the essence of the legal institutions as restricted to those with sufficiently bloated salaries and corporate connections to pay legal bills that easily exceed a poor person's yearly income. The prohibitively high medical costs in the USA are also counter sense objects which communicate the same restriction of the medical industry to those with sufficient corporate connections to be unfazed at the sight of a $600,000 surgery bill which a poor person with no health insurance could not cover even in a lifetime of labouring at three part time jobs. Once again, these are not ideological distortions of some hidden economic truth, as the Marxist would claim: the truth of the legal and medical systems are unambiguously put on display in the form of a bill that accomplishes the social exclusion sought in tens of thousands of pages of systematic complication with a single objective glance. System embodies the notion of system, in a certain sense, precisely in departing from the Gnostic to enter the realm of the Sense Object.

Yet the sense objects are also limited by the limitation of explanation: the counter sense object of a legal bill *presents* the truth of the medical industry as a bloated system that has somehow managed to deliver worse care and riskier services at the same time that its costs have exploded and its body of research and scientific "facts" has grown. The bill presents this truth but it cannot explain it. Counter sense objects are limited by their own inability to critique the counter sense embodied within them, though this is not from a lack of gnostic logical systematicity. Counter sense objects' assault against Reason is a result of the limitation that a counter sense object presents certain pre-linguistic biases in the indirect form of an object understandable only on the basis of such biases. A student loan, for example, is a counter sense object which only seems to make sense because of the implicit faith that the future will always have enough growth later to cover an unpayable bill blindly accepted today. Yet the student loan, as a counter sense object, can never clearly and unambiguously present the bias itself. It can only present what is founded upon this presupposition of growth without ever presenting the presupposition itself. That is why sense objects devolve to utter incomprehensibility when transferred from one worldview to another. The computers, cars, and airplanes so prized today would be curiosities at best to Ancient agrarian thinkers and ugly heaps of trash at worst to Hunter Gatherers in the Ice Age. They will be symbols of evil itself to the Bell Curve thinkers of Decline.

  The deep meme is therefore the determinate limitation to the realm of Sense Objectivity. A deep meme depicting a single infinitely-ascending ray of progress can embody the same worldview much more clearly than the counter sense object of a student loan, machine, $600,000 medical bill, or garbage can. The deep meme presents what the object cannot explain, that these absurdities are just euphemisms for promising that the future will witness enough growth to somehow cover extravagantly high costs today. The deep meme does not need words or even concrete objectivity to explain this. An abstract geometrical metaphor does not even need to be visually seen to influence one's subjective frame of reference. It is not that one literally "sees" the agrarian circle in one's intuition, any more than one literally "sees" the linear ray of progress in one's intuition, as these are memes rather than objects. Yet one can only see an object at all if one has already adopted the memological biases which allow an object to manifest itself in the first place. Even an empirical barrel of petroleum is a counter sense object which must pass through the deep meme of progress which was itself generated by oil in the first place in order to be understood as reduplicating the memological bias of explosive growth and guaranteed surpluses into the indefinite future.

Memes do not escape limitation any more than mythic events, systematic values, or counter sense objects do. Memes' limitation is that although they capture a certain geometrical shape that presents the physical hard limits to survival in a form comprehensible to a subject even in the absence of words, the meme is not itself that resource base. The Soma is the deep meme's determinate limitation insofar as the Soma is what the deep meme is not but the only basis by which the deep meme is what it is. In other words, the Soma is what the deep meme is not but is the only reason that the deep meme is anything at all. The Classical Ancient Greek philosophical question, "Why is there Being at all instead of nothing?" can therefore be rephrased as "What is the limitation which allows a being to be at all rather than be nothing?" If one harbours any doubts about the properly ontological problem of limitation, one should consider whether the deep meme would continue to exist if its somatic basis suddenly vanished. In the absence of fossil fuels, the deep meme of progress will not find itself liberated to finally reach up into the fullness of Being in the absence of the obstacle which had before hindered it; it will find instead that the loss of limitation is literally the loss of Being. Being insofar as it is Being is Limitation.

One might reasonably object that the Soma is given undue privilege in the hierarchy in that there is no deeper layer beyond it which would seem to be its "determinate limitation," holding it in check and taunting its Being with what it is not. Yet this belief would only be valid on the assumption that determinate limitation is the only type of limitation. Beyond the abstract limitation (in the example earlier, simply saying "Superman has limits" without further qualification) and the determinate limitation (saying "Kryptonite is Superman's limitation) lies one more type of limitation. It is incorrect to assume that the Soma itself is some mystical sublime entity with godlike powers, some indestructible substance which only gets stronger with each attack administered against it like Arnold Schwarzenegger's robot in the *Terminator*. The entire point of the present volume has been to warn the reader that the Soma of our era is disappearing rapidly as the author writes these words, and along with it, all the dependent layers of Memology, Counter Sense Objectivity, Gnostic Systematicity, and Mythology which continue to have Being only insofar as they are founded upon the Being of this substance through a relation of limitation. The Soma itself is therefore not free from all limitation. The Soma is not Being itself, like Heidegger's Dasein transposed into the obscure territory of some ontic object like coal or petroleum. The Soma is in itself just another being that must relate to Being through a relation of limitation in order to continue to exist. Yet because there is no deeper layer of determinate limitation beyond which it might relate itself, the Soma is related to Limitation itself through the form of Absolute Limitation.

Absolute Limitation differs from abstract limitation and determinate limitation in the following ways. Abstract limitations merely state the empty tautology that Superman, to return to Jordan Peterson's favourite example, is not what is beyond Superman; his limits are here naively conceived as the dimensional limits of his body which serve as delimiters separating off the outside from the subject. At least within the context of the *Physics*, Aristotle grasped physical limitation through the abstract dimensional delimiters which separate an object from what lies outsides its bodily boundaries. In Book V of *The Physics* Aristotle notes:

> [T]he shortest line is definitely limited [by the endpoints of the line segment], and that which is definitely limited constitutes a measure.[97]

Logically speaking, abstract limitation states that Superman is not not Superman or that a line segment is not the content that lies beyond the interval enclosed by its endpoints, yet each is just an empty positive statement in the guise of a negative statement: in each case, one simply states that $x$ is $x$. Abstract limitation is as impoverished as Hegel's abstract negation.

---

[97] Aristotle, *The Physics* in *Basic Works of Aristotle* (New York: The Modern Library, 2002), p. 307.

Determinate limitation goes beyond abstract limitation by positing the limitation not as the abstract limits of one's body with a simple undifferentiated outside, but rather as the determinate limitation which establishes the limits for what something is by coherently presenting the limitation which it is not. A mythological event is not a systematic value; a systematic value is not a counter sense object; a counter sense object is not a deep meme; a deep meme is not the Soma. Yet one would be mistaken to misread the determinate limitation as a positive obstacle, the removal of which would liberate each to fully claim its Being in unrestricted plentitude and with an unhindered freedom. The loss of determinate limitation also amounts to a loss of Being, not in the absolute sense of a loss of existence but in the minor sense of a loss of essence. The gnostic legal code does not lose all existence when transposed into the counter sense object of an exorbitantly high legal bill for a trivial pseudo-crime; but it does lose its essence as a gnostic value, adopting instead the essence of a counter sense form. Similarly, in the *Cratylus* Plato notes that paradoxical sense in which a picture that exhausted the entire list of attributes of the object it represented would not achieve the status of a "perfect picture." It would instead cease to be a picture altogether; it would instead become just another object:

> I should say rather that the image, if expressing in every point the entire reality, would no longer be an image . . . [If someone captured every feature of Cratylus in a duplicate] would you say that this was Cratylus and the image of Cratylus, or that there were two Cratyluses?[98]

The object is therefore the determinate limitation to the picture: one certainly *could* theoretically duplicate every feature of the object and surpass the limitations of a representation which only captured a partial list of the object's attributes, yet the result would not be a perfect picture: the picture would lose its Being as a picture and would instead leap into a distinct Metaphysical frame and take on

---

[98] Plato, *The Cratylus*, in *Collected Dialogues* (Princeton: Princeton University Press, 1989), p. 466.

the being of an object. Plato's implication, of course, is that the hierarchy of representation would not terminate at this stage either. It would certainly not make any sense to imagine the most "perfect object" being allowed admission into the World of Ideas without sacrificing its Metaphysical status. The object, insofar as it is an object, is inevitably confronted with the Idea in the World of Forms as its own determinate limitation which it could never live up to without ceasing to be an object altogether.

Absolute Limitation differs in that in this case a shift in relation to limitation does not entail a loss of essence, such as a shift from memological essence to somatic essence. Instead, a shift in relation to limitation would entail a loss of existence, and the destruction of the very substance upon which each of the higher order layers was founded as a mere attribute to its underlying Being. Yet even the Soma's relation to Being is not a closed circle of self-relation to itself as some invincible super-substance which generates the whole of existence from out of its privileged position as a First Mover like Thomas Aquinas's or Abu Nasr Al-Farabi's God. Soma relates to limitation as a relation to the Being qua Being which it itself is not. The Soma is not Being: it only exists insofar as it too is given a share of Being which can be removed at any moment. Being is therefore Limitation. The relation between Absolute Limitation and even the Soma which is limited by it is therefore reminiscent of Heidegger's realization of an Ontological Difference in which Dasein could never be understood through even the most sophisticated analysis of the ontic sphere of innerworldly objects because Being is not itself a being. The author's stance differs from Heidegger's most notably in the fact that Heidegger believed that Dasein, the clearing which is its own there, was sufficient to grasp Being. In the present work, on the contrary, the Soma which discloses the five transcendental registers of meaningful revelation is not itself the absolute standard of Being, for it too occupies a finite position with regard to Absolute Limitation and its own possibility to cease to be (a fate which Fossil Fuels are encountering as the author writes these words.)

[1]

| Elements of Field | Determinate Limit to Field |
|---|---|
| Somatic Presence | Absolute Limitation |
| Deep Memological Shape | Soma |
| Sense Objective Form | Deep Meme |
| Systematic Values | Sense Object |
| Mythological Event | Systematic Value |

*Hegel, Plato, Haag*

It is of course important to conclude the present chapter with some remarks on the differences between Haag's Hierarchy of Limitations and Hegel's system of dialectical notions. A naïve viewer might hastily conclude that the present volume is just a Hegelian work in disguise or that the five layers are really just five phases of Notion which dialectically progress from one to the other. This is an understandable temptation but it would defy the deepest philosophical foundation of the present work to accept such a view. One could argue that one of the most important philosophical distinctions in Western History of the division between Plato and Hegel as envisioned by Zizek in *For They Know Not What They Do*. Ironically, both were in agreement over the importance of Notional Thinking as the foundation of Philosophy: they were just in complete disagreement over the ontological status of Notions. Plato's understanding of Notions of course is that they "really exist." Further, the imperfect copies encountered in this world do not have no Being at all so much as they have lesser shares of Being compared to the Idea of which they are the copy. In addition, the movement from a copy of a copy, to a copy, to the Idea does not manifest an equally real degree of Being in each case: Being, rather, *increases* the closer one gets to the Idea. Martin Heidegger's remarks in his lectures on Plato's Cave Allegory are worth repeating:

> [H]e who removes the shackles, says that what is now revealed . . . the things themselves and the human beings, are μᾶλλον ὄντα, *are* to a greater degree [*mehr seined*], are *more beingful* [seiender] beings. What *is* admits of degrees![99]

Hegel's dialectical movement must not be misread as a similar journey from lower to higher degrees of Being. Being, in fact, is *not* the ultimate category situated at the very end of the *Science of Logic*. It is, rather, positioned at the very beginning, as a revelation of its utter primitivity on logical grounds. Yet even at the very beginning one does not find Being in isolation, as though it were some plentitude of positivity like Jean Paul Sartre's "being in itself" which lacks even the tiniest crack into which nothingness might slip.[100] Rather, the Being found at the beginning of Hegel's *Science of Logic* is already found together with negation:

> [T]he beginning is not pure nothing, but a nothing from which something is to proceed; therefore being, too, is already contained in the beginning. The beginning therefore contains both being and nothing, is the unity of being and nothing; or is non-being which is at the same time being, and being which is at the same time non-being.[101]

As Being was already proven at the very beginning of the work to have been contaminated by negation, it would be absurd to suggest that the remainder is a teleological quest for Being. Being does not lie at the end of the journey, as it would for Plato's prisoners released from the Cave to travel through progressively more beingful glimpses into the basis of Being in the Realm of Ideas.[102]

---

[99] See Martin Heidegger's *The Essence of Truth*, p. 29.
[100] Sartre, Jean Paul, *Being and Nothingness* (New York: Washington Square Press, 1984), p. 124.
[101] Hegel, G. W. F., *The Science of Logic* (Kindle Edition).
[102] In Plato's Cave Allegory in the *Republic*, the prisoners are chained up in a cave with their backs to a fire, such that they could only see the shadows on a cave wall cast by the movement of puppets behind their back. The puppets were, in turn, imitations of real entities walking the earth such as horses and men. One day, a prisoner escapes and sees first the puppets, then reflections of real entities in a pool of water, then the horses and men walking the Earth. The story does not conclude there, however, as though these earthly entities were the ultimate standard of Being. Rather, they are themselves revealed to be imperfect copies of the absolute Notions of Horse, Man, Beauty etc. Each of

Hegel's movement differs from Plato's for the additional fact that successive phases in his works do not gain greater and greater immunity to the disease of negation. Later phases are every bit as susceptible to negation; even the final Religion phase of *Phenomenology of Spirit* cannot escape it, as it still fails to embody the Notion perfectly by continuing to portray the Absolute through the Picture Thinking of an exterior entity. Religion treats the Absolute as some transcendent Being and carries over the same kind of Picture Thinking that was present as early as the first section of the *Phenomenology of Spirit*!

For Plato the notions really exist and climbing the stairway to heaven all the way to the top will unearth a pure level of Being that is decidedly not always already negated; but for Hegel, the final layer of Absolute Knowing does not pull back the curtain to reveal Being in a fullness which had been hidden in previous phases. Absolute Knowing, as Zizek is fond of repeating, is simply the formal realization that there really is nothing beyond the inconsistent and contingent movements of dialectic. The Notion is therefore the ultimate intellectual resource to contemplate a level of Being devoid of the fullness promised by Plato's understanding of, ironically enough, the Notion.

It is also crucial to acknowledge the element of temporality. It is true that Hegel's dialectic does not explicitly unfold in any concrete historical time. Those who have tried to interpret the *Phenomenology of Spirit* as a literal history of the world rather than a logical history of the Notion have misunderstood the work considerably. Yet there is also a sense that the sections are not all given in a type of simultaneity whereby the reader might arbitrarily weave in and out of sections at will. It is not that Consciousness, Self-Consciousness, Reason, Spirit, and Religion make up five transcendental registers of meaning among which the subject might consciously shift. In one sense, the lower movements are still available to the higher movements, but only insofar as they are sublated. Heidegger's lectures on Hegel's *Phenomenology of Spirit* demonstrated that the German word *Aufhebung* might be best

---

these Notions existed independently yet none could be understood perfectly without transcending the limitations of earthly things to reach the pure Notion.

understood through its three corresponding Latin terms: *tollere*, to remove or eliminate; *conservare*, to preserve; and *elevare*, to elevate.[103] Hegel chose this triple play on words to emphasize that the previous stages are not conserved as calcified stages which are lined up adjacent to the later stages, such that one could simply travel backwards to view them in their positive coherence. They were only included through being negated, and their preservation could not be thought apart from their negative dissolution as what they once were. Consciousness is, for example, still included in Self-Consciousness and Reason and so forth, but it is only included at the expense of its original identity and mission. No formula of identity could be achieved, equating the Consciousness of Perception of a thing's universal properties with the Consciousness implied in Self-Consciousness's stirring of Life and hunger, or Faust's awakening of sexual desire in the Reason section. Plato preserves each Notion in its self-identity because each Notion is a separate and independent entity; all coexist simultaneously in time and adjacently to one another in the Ideal space of the World of Forms. One can therefore move from one Notion to another without affecting the integrity of each as an entity. One could shift from contemplating Justice to contemplating Beauty to contemplating the Good, as Socrates routinely does in Plato's dialogues, such as the following example from the *Cratylus*:

> There is a matter, Cratylus, about which I often dream, and should like to ask your opinion. Tell me whether there is or is not any absolute beauty or good or any other absolute existence.[104]

Plato is adamant in insisting that these Ideas are *not* in any kind of independent motion, let alone any dialectical motion that would reduce the entire set to the trajectory of a single Notion's imminent movement:

---

[103] Heidegger, Martin, *Hegel's Phenomenology of Spirit* (Bloomington: Indiana University Press, 1994), p. 28.
[104] Plato, *Cratylus*, in *Collected Dialogues* (Princeton: Princeton University Press, 1966), p. 473.

> There is another point I should not like us to be imposed upon by the appearance of such a multitude of names, all tending in the same direction. I myself do not deny that the givers of names really did give them under the idea that all things were in motion and flux, which was their sincere, but, I think, mistaken opinion. And having fallen into a kind of whirlpool themselves, they are carried round and want to drag us in after them.[105]

In this passage Plato suggests that Heraclitus misread flux and motion as the fundamental Metaphysical description of Being due to an optical illusion that misread subjective dizziness and confusion into the essence of the Ideas themselves:

> [T]oo many of our modern philosophers . . . in the search after the nature of things, are always getting dizzy from constantly going round and round, and then they imagine that the world is going round and round and moving in all directions[106]

The Ideas, however, admitted of no motion because motion was just a feature of the imperfect beings on Earth which could not be misread onto the perfect beings in the World of Ideas. Plato does not tend to portray finding motion in one's ideas to be a good thing; it is, rather, a sign of a flawed and confused argument. In the *Euthyphro*, the title character finds that his convictions have grown legs and are wandering away from him even as he is trying all the harder to keep them under control:

> Now Socrates, I simply don't know to tell you what I think. Somehow everything that we put forward keeps moving about us in a circle and nothing will stay where we put it.[107]

---

[105] Ibid.
[106] Ibid., p. 447.
[107] Plato, *Euthyphro*, in *Collected Dialogues* (Princeton: Princeton University Press, 1966), p. 180.

Plato does not mean to suggest that the pure Notions really do wander about incoherently; this motion is just a sign that one has *failed* to penetrate to the realm of Ideal Truth and that one remained at the level of subjective confusion and error. For Hegel, on the other hand, there is no movement without negation and there is no form so solidified as to not lose its identity when swept by negativity. This is arguably one of the most important differences in the history of Western Philosophy.

The author's own stance is irreducible to either of these positions: on the one hand, the five transcendental registers of meaning should not be interpreted as some dialectical progression in which one begins with Mythology and then progresses to System, Sense Objectivity, Meme, and Soma. The Soma is not some end result of a movement that awaits the development of the Notion to manifest its content; the Soma is, rather, the basis upon which the higher layers were always already founded. One does not scale a ladder of Reason to build up the Soma as its final result: the Soma was always already there, insofar as the World in which this movement might occur had to have already been disclosed as a world by the power of the Soma.

On the other hand, it would be equally wrong to think that each of the five layers enjoys the kind of independence from one another which Plato's Ideas have from one another. Mythology is not independent from the lower layers of meaning on which it is founded, as the loss of the Soma would instantaneously result in the destruction of meaning for each of the higher orders of meaning founded upon it. Our contemporary Mythology of the American Dream is already withering into useless untruth as the vast reserves of fossil fuels that made *The Dick Van Dyke Show* seem normal in the 1960's have already declined per capita for the American population: a sitcom in which a young man owns a home in Westchester County, New York, lives with no debt, pays every bill on time, and supports a family on one income as a *writer* would seem like worse than a fairy tale today: it would seem more like a sick joke. Yet this was a perfectly believable and ordinary premise for a sitcom in the 1960's, the last full decade before the United

States hit its own national peak in petroleum production in 1972. This Mythology was not equally independent with the Soma of Fossil Fuels on which it was based, such that in a gallery of Ideas each might be layered in adjacency. Rather, this Mythology simply was the substance of Fossil Fuels manifested within the transcendental structure of a mythic event rather than a systematic value, a sense objective form, a memological shape, or a somatic presence.

In addition to including the lower level of the Soma, Mythology still does imply the other intermediary layers as well. Bitter memories of the Great Depression from just a few short decades earlier are quietly swept under the rug in the *Dick Van Dyke Show*'s universe, with the expectation that a growth in prosperity and a rise in standard of living would continue undisturbed into the indefinite future. This expectation was not an independent mythological datum. It implied each of the lower layers of meaning: the systematic layer of Economic theories favouring continual growth; the counter sense object of a suburban home miles away from the writer's workplace in Manhattan which ruled out walking as an option; the memological shape of an ascending arrow that is easily accommodatable to conservative or political ideologies; and finally, the Soma. Therefore, the author agrees with Hegel's general insight that higher layers include lower ones, though the paradox is that all of them are instantly given together and none of them is dissolved into incoherence by any of the others. Mythology does not disintegrate Soma's substance and devalue it to the status of illusion, as Heidegger claims Hegel's *Phenomenology of Spirit* does to previous phases:

> Phenomenology is not one way among many but *the* manner in which spirit itself exists. The phenomenology of spirit is the genuine and total coming-out of spirit . . . To be a phenomenon, to appear means coming forward in such a way that something shows itself which is other than what previously showed itself, in such a way that what comes forward does so in *opposition* to what previously appeared,

and what previously appeared is reduced to *mere illusion* [Schein][108]

While Hegel certainly did consider that a phase devalued previous forms to the status of illusion, the author's own hierarchy of layers does not unfold over time and does not disintegrate any layer relative to another. There was never any temporal succession in which one had to explicitly generate the higher levels from out of the lower levels. In fact, one does not even begin at the lowest layer of Soma, as one's default stance is always to dwell at the level of Mythology; the journey to Soma requires a Phenomenological stance so carefully-executed that almost no one outside the Peak Oil Community ever manages to penetrate all the way to this deepest foundation of their worldview. The following table summarizes these results. The author agrees more with Plato in temporal terms and more with Hegel in spatial terms but is unique relative to both: [2]

| Thinker | Temporal Dimension | Spatial Dimension |
| --- | --- | --- |
| Plato | Eternal Simultaneity | Adjacency of many independent, coherent Ideas |
| Hegel | Historical Progression | Inclusion of previous forms in higher forms through imminent negation that dissolves coherence |
| Haag | Simultaneity | Inclusion of lower orders in higher orders but integrity of each is maintained rather than dissolved in |

---

[108] Heidegger, Martin, *Hegel's Phenomenology of Spirit* (Bloomington: Indiana University Press, 1994) p. 24.

|  |  | negativity |
|---|---|---|

## *Conclusion*

Abstract, Determinate, and Absolute Limitation could be considered to be the three logical modes by which to contemplate Limitation but the discussion in the present chapter can only serve as a brief introduction to a much more complex issue. The following chapter will continue this discussion of Limitation by demonstrating that the kind of determinate limitation introduced in this chapter (the determinate limitation between one register of meaning and another) is just one of three species of determinate limitation: the transcendent limitation imposed from the outside. Transcendent limitation must be distinguished from transcendental and imminent limitations to provide a fuller account of the precise ontological conditions which allow an appearance to manifest itself in a context far more fragile than one could realize without an appreciation for its dependence on Limitation to exist.

# Chapter Four
# Peak Oil and Existentialist Finitude:
# Against German Idealism and Dialectical Materialism

*German Idealism and Peak Oil: Positivity, Negation, Limitation*

The previous chapter demonstrated that Peak Oil Philosophy must resist the temptation to be submitted under any type of Hegelian Dialectical Philosophy because of the intrinsic difference between negation and limitation. Above all, negation and limitation differ because negation generates a sprawling set of dialectical phases, each of which emerged unpredictably from its predecessor as a testament to dialectic's radical contingency; limitation, on the contrary, forces one to acknowledge that the possible thought forms only appear to be theoretically infinite on the surface level of systematic sprawl or mythological variation but the memological thought-forms, and more importantly the Somatic substance underlying them, are decidedly *not* infinite in variety. Dialectical negation has translated into an unbounded optimism in dialectic's ability to generate literally any historical outcome a person happens to desire. Dialectic is pre-ideological, in that both the Far Left (Socialism, Communism, Maoism) and the Neo-Conservative movements have claimed that their own ideological biases were just the inevitable outcome of a dialectical progression of History. Limitation, on the other hand, does not embody the infinitely-variable morphological flexibility which German Idealism and Dialectical Materialism promised through emphasizing negation. Limitation is precisely what prevents the conceptual elasticity of Truth from exploding into inkblots which later come to be arbitrarily related to the ideology imposed over them with no restriction (or rather, no apparent limitation) over the association between a dead symbol and some content forcibly joined to it. The greatest irony is, of course, that dialectic fell prey to exactly the state of affairs warned about by Hegel from within the perspective of dialectic in his Phrenology section of *Phenomenology of Spirit*. Phrenology follows after the failed attempts by Psychology and

Physiognomy to establish the scientific laws of thought in accord with the notion of Reason as observation. Phrenology follows by radicalizing the "observation" of the bumps on a skull in order to correlate the bumps with personality traits exhibited by the individual. The phrenologist is quickly revealed, however, to have no restriction whatsoever on how the bumps on the skull are interpreted. Association, therefore, devolves to the status of an unrestricted pairing on contents with no intrinsic relation to one another:

> The skull-bone is not an organ of activity . . . Nor has this immediate being the value even of a sign . . . In fact, from whatever side we look at the matter, there is no necessary reciprocal relation at all between [the bumps on the skull and the phenomena they are arbitrarily thought to symbolize], nor any direct indication of such a relation. If, all the same, the relation is still to exist, what remains . . . necessary to form it is an irrational, free, pre-established harmony of the corresponding determination of two aspects . . . On the one hand, we have a multitude of inert areas of the skull, on the other, a multitude of mental properties.[109]

The author will argue that overemphasizing negation intrinsically opens a pathway for an unrestricted (or rather, un-limited) arbitrariness in interpretation because, after all, to negatively say that something is not something else is even less restricted in content than affirming that something is something determinate. Limitation is much more difficult to understand than negation because understanding that something is not something else is relatively easy; that is Abstract Limitation. Understanding that something is limited by something else is much harder; that is Determinate Limitation. Understanding that something is limited by Limitation itself has arguably been left unachieved thus far; that is Absolute Limitation. For all of its brilliance, German Idealism will not provide access to this pathway. A deep meditation on Limitation

---

[109] Hegel, G. W. F., *Phenomenology of Spirit* (Oxford: Oxford University Press, 1977), pp. 200-202.

will not provide fuel for the fire of unbounded hope in revolutionary changes, however implausible or ideologically-loaded: limitation will rather provide an ontological basis for the existentialist concept of finitude, the acceptance of one's thrownness into a historically contingent situation one did not choose, in a life that decidedly will end in death, within a horizon of meaning that is only temporarily disclosed from the Soma which will soon meets its own resource death through depletion.

Dialectical Negation accommodates itself easily to figures from completely incompatible perspectives because it has an inherent morphological flexibility which positivity and limitation both lack. Each of these deserve brief consideration before proceeding. Virtually no one consciously espouses a Metaphysics of Positivity, though in one form of another it might be considered to be the naïve, pre-philosophical stance towards reality that has not yet factored in more sophisticated notions of negation or limitation. This Positivity without negation or limitation is roughly the stance of the Dogmatist, the hypothetical opponent attacked so frequently in Fichte's early writings. In his first introduction to the *Wissenschafteslehre*, Fichte argues that ultimately, every person will hold only one of the following two positions with regard to the grounds of experience:

> [One either] thus retains the [I] in itself, or the "Thing in itself," as the explanatory ground of Experience. The former mode of proceeding is called Idealism, the latter Dogmatism. Only these two philosophical systems—and of that these remarks should convince everybody—are possible. According to the first system the representations, which are accompanied by the feeling of necessity, are productions of the Intelligence, which must be presupposed in their explanation; according to the latter system they are the productions of a thing in itself which must be presupposed to explain them.[110]

---

[110] Fichte, Johann Gottlieb, "First Introduction to the *Wissenschaftslhere*," in *Works of Johann Gottlieb Fichte*, Kindle Edition.

Fichte himself considered this to be more of a false choice than a genuine dilemma, since the Thing in Itself posited by the Dogmatist as the foundation of experience was actually just a fiction:

> The object of Dogmatism . . . [was] produced solely by free Thinking. The Thing in itself is a mere invention, and has no reality at all.[111]

Fichte resisted grounding his system in a Thing in Itself because this fiction, if it did exist, would radically preclude subjective freedom. Dogmatist Metaphysics would present Being as a closed-off, solidified objectivity devoid of even the possibility of a radical act of the subject that could intervene and freely determine reality in accord with the will. Fichte's opposition to the Metaphysics of Dogmatic Positivity was so radical that he was not even content to consider the mind to be a "free thing" or an object with the freedom to act: rather, he considered the mind to be in itself an activity. This freedom would later be considered in German Idealism to be negation.

It is no coincidence that some of the earliest writings in German Idealism already portray a crass Metaphysics of Positivity as the antithesis to German Idealism's radicalization of freedom and of the Act. A reductive Metaphysics of Positivity, of course, would simply equate the present state of achieved outcomes with the potential set of possibilities for the future. In other words, the overlap between appearance and Being would be so full that no possibilities could emerge that would contradict the current state of affairs. "What is" would be considered to be so conclusively settled that there would be no conceptual space for "what is not" to disrupt the static givenness of positive Being.

The reader may have legitimate doubts about whether the present work is itself just a type of Dogmatic Philosophy which Fichte dismissed so heatedly. This an understandable result of the author's insistence that it is the Soma itself, not Dasein, which discloses the horizon of mythological meaningfulness in which the

---

[111]Ibid.

existential subject always already finds himself or herself absorbed; this may at first glance sound uncomfortably close to how Fichte described the Myth of Dogmatism:

> According to the Dogmatist, all phenomena of our consciousness are productions of a Thing in Itself, even our pretended determinations by freedom, and the belief that we are free. This belief [in freedom] is produced by the effect of the Thing in Itself upon ourselves[112]

The author acknowledges that it would be all too easy to misread the author's notion of Soma as just another dogmatic emphasis on the Thing in Itself of Fossil Fuels generating the subject's thought forms as a secondary side effect of the Soma's influence which is later misread by the subject as its own intellectual freedom to think. However, this would only be valid if one interpreted the present volume through a tacit Marxist or Materialist standpoint, in which case the higher order layers would be devalued to mere "ideological reflections" of the underlying Material Base of Fossil Fuels. It is all too rarely acknowledged that Fichte himself designated the *materialist* as the ultimate dogmatist and described his opponent as someone very similar to the figure which Marx eventually came to realize:

> [C]onsistent dogmatism . . . thus becomes materialism- the soul to them is no Thing at all, and indeed nothing at all, but merely a production, the result of the reciprocal action of Things amongst themselves. But this reciprocal action produces merely a change in the Things and by means anything apart from the Things.[113]

Fichte's description of the Dogmatist reducing consciousness and its ideas to secondary effects of relations amongst the things is of course a very close description to what Marx later designated as the tendency for subjects to misread relations within the material base

---

[112] Ibid.
[113] Ibid

for their own subjective illusions which were merely an ideological distortion of the impersonal movement of Things within the Material Base. For this reason, it is all the more bizarre that Zizek tends to argue that each of the German Idealists was really a materialist in disguise, despite their obvious insistence to the contrary.[114]

At any rate, the author's view of Soma could only appear to be a Dogmatist Philosophy if one implicitly accepted that the Soma is akin to the Material Base and that Mythology is just Ideology generated secondarily by the agency of material conditions. First of all, the author has already made clear that Soma must not be confused with objectivity: objectivity is, in itself, just a higher order register of meaning which can only be constituted on the basis of its own foundedness on the Soma. Marx's supposed descent to the depths of the Material Base only ever reached the intermediary layer of the sense object of industrial machinery; in Heidegger's view, he only ever reached the capitalist mode of production as an object present at hand and neglected to notice the more primordial foundation of Understanding which had to account for this object's givenness as a meaningful something in the first place. Second of all, the author has never suggested that Mythology is just an ideological illusion which can never be transcended, since, as Zizek is fond of repeating, the claim to transcend ideology is itself the most perfect example of an ideological statement. Mythology does not hide the Soma behind a curtain in which one becomes even more entangled the more one tries to go beyond it, in that the claim to go beyond Mythology would be itself the most profoundly mythological statement. Rather, the author has made it clear that Mythology can quite easily be transcended since it is only one of five registers of meaning. The Soma is not some ineffable, inaccessible X which can only be restored indirectly from our flawed and ideologically-biased horizon of subjective illusion: the Soma is, rather, just the deepest layer in a hierarchy which a

---

[114] In addition to giving the title *Less Than Nothing: Hegel and the Shadow of Dialectical Materialism* to his 900 page book on Hegel, Zizek titled an entire section of his book on Schelling "The Materialist Notion of the Subject". See *The Indivisible Remainder* p. 70.

sufficiently responsibly conducted Phenomenological approach can in fact reach. Further, if one finds oneself dwelling in the horizon of the mythological event or any of the other higher order registers of meaning, then one need not seek out the Soma in some distant region: the Soma is already there. Its relation to Mythology and the higher order registers is more like the Ancient Greek relation between substance and accident than the relation between Thing in Itself and appearance or between Material Base and Ideology. In the case of substance, the substance is already presumed in any of its higher order categories, for the higher categories are intelligible only insofar as they are founded upon some substance. Shuffling among the ten classical categories does not generate ten different objects or, in the worst case, nine objects which are merely distortions of a single inaccessible base. They are, rather, just the same substance given in ten different categorical headings of meaning. The Soma is not outside the intuition of Mythology, System, Sense Object, or Deep Meme: the Soma simply is the substance underlying each of these but is therefore really "there" in the intuition no matter which layer is given.

Ancient Greek Philosophy and the Phenomenology to which it is closely related differ from German Idealism in that in German Idealism the appearance is largely an appearance devoid of substance (either because the substance is beyond it as Thing in Itself or because there is no substance at all so much as there are unstable forms which only ever obtain an illusory level of stability relative to the radical negation which will later sweep them into irrelevance); but in Phenomenology and Ancient Greek Philosophy an appearance is a true appearance only insofar as it has substance *within* it. In Ancient Greek Philosophy the substance is not somewhere beyond the appearance; rather, substance is already there in the intuition, even if given only vaguely and incoherently at first or obscured under some categorical heading which explicitly privileges a higher order category as the standard of meaning. The promise of clarifying the intuition to reach the substance within it must not be thought of as an act that seeks some content lying decidedly on the outside of the appearance. It is rather, a clarification of the content that was always already there in the first appearance. Fossil Fuels are not somewhere on the outside of, say, Elon Musk's ridiculous plans to escape from the pollution his own industry generates by fleeing to Mars: even the most unclear intuition of Elon Musk's preposterous plans contains the substance of Fossil Fuels which provide the only rationale to make this insanity pass for "brilliance."

In the next phase of German Idealism, Schelling followed after Fichte by presenting an even more sophisticated meditation on the incompatibility between freedom and a Metaphysics of Positivity. Under Schelling, German Idealism called into question the primacy not only of the Thing in Itself, but even of the established order of Nature in which the subject would seem to be just another link in the organic chain of natural beings. Above all, Schelling was interested in the philosophical question of how freedom could exist in a natural world which appeared to the naïve viewer to be a closed-off, determined totality ordered both spatially within Nature and temporally within History. Schelling's response was to reveal that the subject's freedom is not some anomalous excess of negation that intrudes into the established order of positive Being through some inexplicable event with no basis beyond the subject. Rather, Schelling argued that a "free subject" overlaps with the "pure freedom" of God because the established order of a positively-ordered Creation is not primary: it is the result of God's decision to abruptly transform chaos into order and transition from eternity to temporality.[115] In other words, the positive Being of creation is not an absolute given: it is a secondary result which follows from a more primordial pre-creation horizon which was dominated by the "rotary motion of pulsating drives" (somewhat comparable to Freud's notion of the unconscious drives) which provided the fundamental antagonism which God sought to overcome by establishing a created order.[116] Even if his emphasis is less explicitly placed on negation than Hegel's, Schelling's view that the positive Being of creation is *not* freedom clearly places an emphasis on freedom as something which is out of joint with the

---

[115] Zizek, Slavoj, *The Indivisible Remainder: On Schelling and Related Matters* (London: Verso, 1996), p.34.
[116] Ibid., p. 33.

positive order which is itself just a secondary side effect of the Act of a God with the ultimate non-positive freedom to act.

Of course, the author acknowledges that there is enormous intellectual wealth to be found in German Idealism; in fact, the present work would not have been possible without some influence from Fichte, Schelling, and Hegel that has not even been given its due acknowledgment thus far. However, the author sees no value at all in importing inspiration from any of the Dialectical Materialist schools of thought to craft a solution to Peak Oil. In fact, trying to devise a Communist response to Peak Oil would literally be as self-contradictory as trying to devise a Capitalist response to Peak Oil, since both ideologies fall under the spell of the Deep Meme of Progress by mistaking the counter sense object of the machine for the Soma of Fossil Fuels which provide its unspoken possibility precisely through serving as its deepest determinate limitation. Above all else, the present work must not be read as a materialist (and especially not a Marxist) piece of Philosophy.

*Earth: The New Arrakis*

Whereas Marxists tend to envision concern with resources as a fixation on the materialist objectivity of, say, modes of production, the author proposes that such an approach misses the point that survival hinges far more on the mysterious notion of limitation than on the more easily-accessible notion of physical materialism, even a materialism into which some vague notion of negation has been smuggled by the sophists. Herbert's cryptic novel *Dune* argues that far more important than the systematic knowledge which machines have become so skilled at employing is the contemplation of limitation, a concept which machines are arguably utterly at a loss to arrive at, since they are restricted to pursuing paths of systematic exploration alone, in which the only determinate pathway for thought is to proceed from one value to another value. Even values which supposedly represent nothingness or the lack of value must themselves embody some particular value. For the computers, the number zero is not actually "nothing" so much as it is a determinate pseudo-numerical electrical value which can only represent the absence of value symbolically. The binary signature for "zero" is a symbol for the absence of value but it is in itself still a positive value. Further, this "zero" is not nothing at all because it is only possible if the machine is switched on and connected to an electrical energy source. Even the "off state" is truly just an "on state" in disguise. Computers are even more incapable of representing limitation. Cheating by representing a limit as the "final" value in a list or as the negation of value such as "zero" would only prove machines' enslavement to schemas of systematic value which are by definition incapable of representing a limit as such.

*Dune* portrays the understanding of limitation as literally a life or death matter, as its setting on the desert planet Arrakis centres on the limitation of water: water on Arrakis is not some objective positivity to be taken for granted or contemplated in its plentitude of givenness, as the materialist rationalist would claim. Water is, rather, something which is so limited that a neglect of its limitation will guarantee nothing except a quick death, a fate which even the most scrupulous and cautious resident may still fail to avoid. Measures to preserve every single drop of water border on the ridiculous:

> He found his stillsuit's watertube in its clip at his neck, drew a warm swallow into his mouth, and he thought that here he truly began an Arrakeen existence- living on reclaimed moisture from his own breath and body. It was flat and tasteless water, but it soothed his throat.[117]

The most interesting thing about *Dune*, however, is that it does not portray this lack of water through the materialist cliché of material deprivation inhibiting rational growth (the politically correct myth that the only reason for conflict is that an insufficient number of people have been "lifted up" into an American upper middle class suburban lifestyle.) Rather than inhibit one's spiritual and intellectual growth, living under limitation is the only thing that can

---

[117] Herbert, Frank, *Dune* (New York: Ace Books, 1990), p. 204.

allow one access to enduring wisdom over academic fashionableness:

> 'I've heard a saying,' Paul said, 'that polish comes from the city, wisdom from the desert.'[118]

Certainly, living in the era of Peak Oil offers us a similar opportunity to achieve wisdom through contemplating Limitation which could never be achieved through running ever more laps through the rat maze of academic fads, an activity for which the unstated teleological goal of securing a high salary and prestigious job vastly overshadow any real concern for achieving wisdom. *Dune* suggests that wisdom arises from the desert because wisdom is not just the positive correlate to some objective state of affairs, nor is it even the negation of positivity: wisdom is the intellectual confrontation with Limitation which can be reduced neither to positivity nor negativity.

A perceptive reader might be at a loss to explain why the planet Earth in the year 2019 is not treating petroleum the way that residents of Arrakis treat water. In both cases, ignorance of limitation will lead to nothing except a painful and early death; the author is not speaking figuratively here. One measure for how incapable we are of giving the limitation of oil its due is the utter insanity represented by the fact that Nascar, one of the most popular sports in the United States, requires some 5,375 gallons of gasoline to be burned just to finish *one* race of the 36 or so which are conducted each year. The 193,500 gallons of gasoline required just to finish out one season and crown a champion who will be completely forgotten even by the time the next season begins can easily be taken for granted in a world where fuel prices seem negligible enough to make energy seem, for all intents and purposes, free. Yet it would be hard to imagine this scale of energy waste to be regarded so casually by future generations who will likely live in a world far closer to Arrakis than Bush's, Obama's, or Trump's America.

---

[118] Ibid., p.145.

Admittedly, a Nascar fan could legitimately point out that the 5,375 gallons burned to drive circles around the same track all afternoon at one race is so microscopic a fraction of the 360,000,000 gallons of gas used daily in the USA that it is unfair to single Nascar out as though it were some uniquely evil contributor to this disease. Regardless of how the share of blame works out mathematically, one thing is quite certain: the folk mythology of the future will not be kind to Nascar. Just as in the post-Roman era the Coliseum came to stand as a symbol of Rome's decadence, in which gladiators fought to the death and Christians were killed by "exotic" animals shipped from remote locations in Africa, the agrarian peasants of the far future will likely view the vast abandoned Nascar tracks in North Carolina and New Hampshire with the same disgust and moral condemnation as a Medieval Christian would level against Roman blood sport.

The residents of the far future who recount legends of the wicked Oil Era Past will not be corporate office drones, comfortably-tenured professors, or professional usurers. They will be shepherds whose flocks will graze on the ruins of the campuses in Silicon Valley that remain above the encroaching Pacific Ocean; blacksmiths who repurpose metal pipes salvaged from the tattered scraps of once-prosperous suburban cul-de-sacs; fishermen who sail simple fishing boats deep enough into the Atlantic Ocean to bypass the toxic waters near the coast while reciting legends about how the wicked island of Manhattan (faintly visible as a set of decaying towers rising up over the horizon) came to be buried under water as a punishment for serving as the usury capital of the world; grain farmers whose horses or oxen will plough reclaimed urban spaces for purposes far more useful than corporate office space; and potters who will load their goods onto donkey carts and tread rocky paths from the rural hinterlands to the town to barter with customers in need of pots for cooking and winemaking. The fact that these social roles are literally unthinkable to the upper middle class chair-warmers who will recoil in ghastly horror and disgust at the thought of having to get their hands dirty with physical labour is only confirmation that it is not enough to call the difference between them and their peasant descendants a "subjective difference." A far more precise term is needed: this will be a Memological difference based upon a Somatic difference, which is in turn based upon a direct relation to the Absolute Limitation which limits even the Soma to a type of finitude in the face of its own possibility of non-existence.

## *Limitation and Finitude*

The author's vehement rejection of Materialism may seem inconsistent with the emphasis thus far on grounding Peak Oil Philosophy in the somatic substance of Fossil Fuels in our era, agrarian grain in the Medieval and Ancient eras, megafauna herds in the Prehistoric eras, and salvage in the future. Under the naïve view, reducing Mythology, Systems, Sense Objects, and even Deep Memes to their substantial basis in the Soma would seem to be just another type of reduction of ideological epiphenomena to their materialist base. In this case, one would argue that "nothing really exists at all" except for the Soma, misunderstood as some type of material object stripped of the illusory meanings that had been arbitrarily layered on top of it. This claim, however, could only be justifiable if the author had stated that Soma is literally the only type of substance that could exist. In fact, the author has not even claimed that the hierarchy of five registers of meaning (somatic, memological, sense objective, systematic, mythological) is the only conceivable hierarchy of meanings that could exist. The author simply stated that for the human subjects who are reading this text, the hierarchy of meanings grounded in the substance of Soma is the only one transcendentally available to us. The materialist hastily concludes that his or her own transcendental structures of meaning are sufficient to account for the totality of truth, in that no other frames could be assumed to exist. The existentialist, on the other hand, accepts that absolute certainty would be absurd to strive for even within the native territory of the framework of consciousness which *is* readily available to the subject, let alone within any totalizing picture of all existence. The present work is therefore far more in line with Kierkegaard than Hegel and far more in line with Heidegger than Marx. The conflict between Existentialism and

Dialectic remains one of the most significant intellectual battles of our era, and the present work, while not exactly a piece of Existentialism, will certainly acknowledge that the concept of Finitude will hold the key to unlocking why Peak Oil Philosophy must not be subordinated to any Materialism.

The most immediate meaning of Finitude in Existentialism is of course that the human subject is not an absolute intelligence floating in an idealistic vacuum populated solely by the abstract eternal truths; instead, the human subject is quite literally finite, insofar as if subjectivity is given it all, it is always already limited as "being toward death."[119] In addition to being limited by an impending death which can never be overcome, the human subject is also limited by the contingency of having to exist as thrown into a situation one did not choose, a situation further obfuscated by the temptation to fall into the anonymous idle chatter of the crowd rather than awaken to the existentialist call for authenticity which would require acknowledging one's being towards death as an individual predicament for which no one else can substitute responsibility.

Likewise, Existentialist Philosophy was built on revolutionizing the meaning of the term "existence" itself. Often, the term is misinterpreted to mean something like objective presence. When one asks whether Bigfoot or the Loch Ness Monster exists, one means to ask whether there is an object in the world which could be made present to a subject who discovered it. One could even speak this way about the existence of inanimate objects, such as whether ruins of an Ancient Civilization might still exist deep within the mountains. In this sense, existence would be intelligible solely within the naïve Metaphysics of Positivity, in which positive givenness as an object would be sufficient grounds to establish existence even in the absence of subjective reflection upon one's existence.

Existentialist Philosophy differed from this stance by arguing that only the aware subject exists.[120] This is not to deny that

---

[119] Heidegger, Martin, *Being and Time* (Albany: State University of New York Press, 1996), p. 216.

[120] Admittedly, when Heidegger says that only Dasein exists he is careful to

inanimate objects are real; it is rather to argue that only a being which is concerned about its being can truly qualify as one that exists. For Jean Paul Sartre the distinction between an object with no concern for its being, like a table, and a subject with an awareness of its existence required an ontological separation between Being and Nothingness: it was not that the consciousness of an existing subject was a specific kind of objective being who was still a member of the same genus populated by tables and rocks. It was, in fact, not even proper to call it a positive being at all: Sartre found instead that it was most proper to describe consciousness as a nothingness. He reached this conclusion from accepting Husserl's theory of Intentionality but following it to its extreme logical conclusion: if consciousness is consciousness *of* the object itself rather than a theatre of representation filled with an illusory appearance, then consciousness must itself be so directed towards the object that it is, in itself, nothing. Therefore, logical negation, freedom, and bad faith could only emerge in a world mostly populated by inanimate objects if they emerged from within a consciousness which was itself negative, a consciousness which was nothing rather than a determinate something.[121] However, if freedom emerged from nothingness, then it was intrinsically unlimited. Sartre's "proof" for the non-existence of God was that if a God existed, he would provide a limitation to the subject's freedom; but because the subject's freedom is inherently a nothing rather than a something, such a limit would be impossible to impose upon this freedom. In addition, avoiding limitations on one's own freedom imposed at the political level allowed Sartre to rationalize revolutionary violence under the belief that if freedom is absolute (or more specifically, unlimited) then it must be fought for, however catastrophic the results.

---

qualify this by saying that Dasein must not be equated with a subject, a life, or even a person, but the general sketch of a subject existing is more useful to link Heidegger, Dostoyevsky, Sartre, and Kierkegaard than to try to fit the latter thinkers into some notion of Dasein which they did not know of. Heidegger, Martin, *Being and Time* (Albany: State University of New York Press, 1996), p. 39.
[121] Sartre, Jean Paul, *Being and Nothingness* (New York: Washington Square Press, 1984), p. 119.

Sartre's view was therefore not terribly far from Fichte's conclusion reached as early as the 18th Century at the dawn of German Idealism. Both Sartre and Fichte resisted the Dogmatism of a Thing in Itself by radicalizing the freedom of a subject through opposing negation to crass positivity. Despite the label of existentialist, therefore, Sartre failed to grasp Limitation and remained a German Idealist in the guise of an Existential Phenomenologist.

Martin Heidegger's *Being and Time* was considerably more carefully-worded and more cautiously-reasoned-out than anything Sartre produced; Heidegger extended this methodological caution to his analysis of freedom in the context of finitude and death. A full treatment of his analysis of these three topics is simply beyond the scope of the present discussion, but one notable difference between him and Sartre is that Heidegger never suggests that the subject's freedom is so absolute that it would a priori rule out the existence of even the slightest limitation upon it. Dasein is not some abstract subjective agency with an unrestricted power to transform the world according to a groundless vision as a proof of its "radical negativity." Dasein is, rather, first and foremost thrown into an historical contingency it did not choose, in the midst of the idle chatter of *Das Man* (the They) which obscures even its own ability to recognize itself for what it is:

> And only because Dasein, in understanding is its there, can it go astray and fail to recognize itself. And since understanding is attuned and attunement is existentially surrendered to thrownness, Dasein has always already gone astray and failed to recognize itself. In its potentiality of being, it is thus delivered over to the possibility of first finding itself again in its possibilities.[122]

The most important thing which Dasein's tendency to get lost in the They obfuscates is the meaning of its own incompleteness by trivializing Death into an ontic occurrence which

---

[122]Heidegger, Martin, *Being and Time* (Albany: State University of New York Press, 1996), p. 135.

always occurs to somebody else, rather than as a testament to the paradoxical sense in which as Care, Dasein is always ahead of itself yet is unable to ever fully catch up to itself in that the final outstanding remainder of Death is something which precisely will not occur to it as an ontic event that can be meaningfully disclosed. Thus, death is not an anonymous misfortune that happens to someone else or to no one in particular: death is, rather, completely Dasein's own and is in fact what forces Dasein back onto it's ownmost potentiality-of-being.[123] The They fundamentally inhibit Dasein from reaching authenticity because death's revelation of Dasein's incompleteness is instead obscured by the They, as the They misrecognizes death as a real ontic occurrence which is no one's in particular:

> The publicness of everyday being-with-one-another 'knows' death as a constantly occurring event, as a 'case of death.' Someone or another 'dies,' be it a neighbour or stranger . . . [But d]ying is levelled down to an event which does concern Dasein, but which belongs to no one in particular. If idle talk is always ambiguous, so is this way of talking about death . . . It treats it as something always already 'real' and veils its character as possibility.[124]

But because death does not actually occur to Dasein as an event, death is not a mundane object which can be grasped through the traditional categories which presume an entity which is present at hand. Yet death is also not an ineffable mystical being which Dasein cannot relate to through its attuned understanding. Dasein's being-towards-death is, rather, the familiar Existentialist concept of Angst.[125] Perhaps unexpectedly, Heidegger's locates Dasein's freedom in the context of Angst and therefore, death:

---

[123] Ibid., p. 232.
[124] Simultaneously, "Angst belongs to [Dasein's] self-understanding in terms of its ground."
Ibid., p. 234 and p. 245

> Anticipation reveals to Dasein its lostness in the they-self and brings it face to face with the possibility to be itself, primarily unsupported by . . . taking care of things, but to be itself in passionate anxious freedom toward death which is free of the illusions of they, factical, and certain of itself.[126]

The most notable difference between Sartre and Heidegger is therefore that whereas Sartre largely implies that freedom is the result of the subject's intrinsic ontological character as a Nothingness which is so negative that no positive being-in-itself could pose an obstacle to it except through some subjective illusion which would be quite easily negated away, Heidegger does not portray Dasein's freedom through the German Idealist resources of negation so much as he presents freedom as Dasein's paradoxical relation to its own limitation in death. It is only because Dasein is not just empirically limited but *fundamentally* limited by death that Dasein responds to its own "possibility of . . . absolute impossibility" with a freedom in the face of its own limitation.[127]

Heidegger therefore presented one of the most important philosophical meditations on the notion of limitation in the context of its properly ontological implications for Being's possibility of ceasing to be. However, Heidegger did not consider this limitation to be in itself the ontological meaning of Being, which he reserved for Dasein and its fundamental structures as a clearing which discloses itself without the mediation of some extrinsic Soma. The limitation of death was, rather, something which Dasein had to relate to either authentically or inauthentically by either facing it as its own or by retreating into the obfuscation of the They-Self.

It is crucial to note, though, that he favoured using the word "absolute" to describe the limitation to which Dasein relates through its being-toward-death: although Dasein's stance toward death must be its own, since no one can die for another, he does not mean to present death as a merely relative limitation but rather insists that it is the "possibility of . . . absolute impossibility" which Dasein must face in its authentic freedom towards death. In the

---

[126] Ibid.
[127] Ibid., p. 232.

author's own terminology, one could say that Heidegger implied that Dasein was faced with Absolute Limitation in death, in that the death did not represent the limitation of any one particular ability or feature, but rather the limit to existence itself, beyond which nothing except the utter darkness of non-being lay.

Heidegger's emphasis on Dasein's relation to Absolute Limitation must be resolved with the author's claim in the previous chapter that the Soma, lacking any determinate limitation to structure its criteria of intelligibility from a lower level, was the sole layer in the hierarchy of five which directly related to the Absolute Limitation since there was no layer deeper than it. Where, after all, does the subject fit within this hierarchy? Does the existential subject relate to Absolute Limitation through the prospect of death, or is this merely an incomplete euphemism for the Soma's unique relation to Being and Non-Being, to which no other entity can lay claim?

## *The Incredible Shrinking Existentialist Man*

The author acknowledges Heidegger's enormous contribution to the philosophical investigation of limitation in death; however, the author would suggest that Heidegger's insight into death might be fit into the context of an Ontology of Limitation rather than an Ontology of Dasein. In the process, the author shall address the most pressing ambiguity implied thus far in the text: where, exactly, within the hierarchy of transcendental registers of meaning does the subject fit? Can the subject be located somatically, memologically, sense objectively, gnostically, or mythologically? Or is the subject just a neutral super-layer which pre-exists all of these frames and merely alternates from one to the other at will? Is the subject a fiction with no existence at all? Or are there five subjects, each of which is wedded to its respective layer but has no endurance or existence beyond the span of time that that particular layer is put into action?

Answering this question is of course impossible without an ontological clarification with regard to the Being of this subject. The previous chapter demonstrated that Limitation remains one of the most under-explored territories in all of Philosophy. Part of the difficulty has stemmed from the inherent ambiguity with regard to whether one is speaking of a relative limitation which cannot be understood independently of the object of which it is the limit or whether one is speaking about an absolute limitation with no intrinsic relation to a subject or object. Even distinguishing relative from absolute limitation, as the previous chapter did, is not sufficient to provide a rigorous system for grasping an Ontology of Limitation, let alone the subject's own mysterious role within it.

The author would argue that relational limitation is an abstract notion which cannot be instantiated concretely without falling into a specific mode. There are, in total, three modes of relative limitation, corresponding to Philosophy's traditional modes of imminence, transcendence, and the transcendental.

One of the more regrettable facts in the History of Western Philosophy is that "transcendent" and "transcendental" are words so easily confused despite being completely different. For this reason, the author will first clarify what each of these terms means. First, imminence refers to contents that are within. Hegel revolutionized the Philosophy of Truth by claiming that truth is not an agreement between the subject's mind and some transcendent arrangement of objects in the real world; truth was rather to be measured on the grounds of Imminent Critique in which the Notion could be evaluated for whether it had lived up to its own criteria or if it had already failed to be itself (just as the colloquial phrase "true gold" asks after the imminent relation of the gold to itself to determine whether it is true or fool's gold.)

Second, the transcendent refers to something from the outside; a transcendent object might be, for example, a cow in a field that has an independent existence as an object. The great mystery of Philosophy has been how consciousness can leave itself to become aware of something transcendent to itself.

Finally, the transcendental differs from the transcendent in that the transcendental *is not* an object with an independent existence and endurance beyond the subject. Kant understood space and time, for example, to be transcendental features of the subject's ability to process sense contents meaningfully; but space and time were not "real" transcendent givens with an independent existence beyond the subject.

One might suggests that these three make up the general modes of relation. Even a relation as fundamental as limitation is either imminent, transcendent, or transcendental if it is not considered as absolute. The previous chapter focused on only one type of determinate limitation, the transcendent limitation that holds between one layer of meaning and another which is outside it. The present chapter will focus, in addition, on imminent and transcendental limitation.

Once again, a determinate limitation between a higher order layer of meaning and the lower order of meaning on which it is founded is a transcendent limitation. In Hegel's *Philosophy of Mind*, when Art finally ceases to fail to embody its own notion, it does not become Perfect Art: it becomes Religion. When Religion ceases to fail to be Religion, it does not become Perfect Religion: it becomes Philosophy. One could say that Religion is Art's transcendent determinate limitation and that Philosophy is Religion's. Similarly, in Plato's *Cratylus*, a perfect representation of an object is not a perfect representation; it is a just an object. The object is not some imminent content which obstructs the representation. It is rather the transcendent limitation which, precisely when it is reached, causes the representation to lose its Being insofar as its Being always already was limitation. It only existed insofar as it was limited by the determinate limitation. Similarly, in Ancient and Medieval Religion, a perfect man is not a perfect man: he is a god. A perfect woman is not a perfect woman: she is a goddess. Even as early as *The Iliad*, this paradoxical relation between humans and their determinate limitation, the gods and goddesses, was understood:

> When Aeneas saw [Diomed] thus making havoc among the ranks, he [wondered if] he [were] some god who [was] angry with the Trojans about their sacrifices, and [had] set his hand against them in his displeasure.[128]

---

[128] Homer, *The Iliad* (New Delhi: Fingerprint! Classics, 2017), p.63.

Diomed's power in Book V was of course not his own but was just Minerva's supernatural aid extended to him through a veil of obfuscation which the mortal men could not penetrate. The gods themselves, however, understood Diomed's subordinate position to them quite well and when Diomed recklessly turned to attacking the gods themselves who were fighting for the Trojans he was warned by Apollo:

> When [Diomed] was coming on for the fourth time, as though he were a god, Apollo shouted to him with an awful voice and said, 'Take heed, son of Tyedus, and draw off: think not to match yourself against gods, for men that walk the earth cannot hold their own against immortals.'[129]

Apollo is Diomed's transcendent determinate limitation which prevents him from conclusively being what he is but whose limitation is the sole thing that sustains him in his Being, since a man that ceased to be limited by the god, by catching up with the god and becoming one himself, would cease to be a man. In Christianity, Jesus Christ was not a perfect man so much as he was God. This is not a loss of all being so much as a loss of a certain type of being as established through the determinate limitation of a transcendent limit.

The author accepts Hegel's, Plato's, and Homer's examples as legitimate instantiations of transcendent determinate limitation but argues that these are all empirical examples with a contingent or a posteriori nature. One could go beyond empirical examples of transcendent determinate limitation to find the purified a priori transcendent limitations which hold not just between two particular objects with empirical content but rather between different a priori layers of meaningfulness as disclosed within the five layers of Mythology, System, Sense Object, Deep Meme, and Soma. These provide the transcendent limitation not only of particular examples of meaning but rather for general horizons of meaning themselves.

---

[129] Ibid., p. 68.

For example, Homer only explicitly demonstrates a relation between two contents (i.e., the mortal Diomed, the god Apollo) within the field of Mythology. But Mythology itself has its own transcendent determinate limitation which allows it to be Mythology by revealing that Mythology is Mythology only insofar as it is not System. Mythology is inherently limited by its own vagueness. The mythological layer can overcome its own poetical ambiguity and hermeneutical inconclusiveness but only by short-circuiting its transcendent relation to the determinate limitation of systematic value. When Mythology becomes System, it overcomes inconclusiveness on the micro-level of the unit, in that a mythic event as a unit is unclear but systematic value as a unit is clear. However, the system then transfers its limitation to inconclusiveness at the level of a full system. One particular symbol within the Google Algorithm, such as the number "1" or the conjunction logical operator "&&" is clear but the system as a whole still states unclearly in billions of symbols what can be presented clearly in a single, coherent counter sense object. The machine communicates the ideology, memological biases, and somatic substance which the Google Algorithm strives to present but does so in one single intuition rather than have it be deferred over a sprawling system of symbolic mediations which somehow never succeed in reaching the "final value." Yet the counter sense object suffers its own transcendent limitation and incompleteness by transferring inconclusiveness to the level of geometrical purification. Oswald Spengler's obsession with restoring the geometrical bias of ascension from the sense object of the Faustian Cathedral or restoring the Magian geometrical shape of a layout of conflict from the sense object of an astrological catalogue of stars demonstrated that a single sense object or counter sense object achieves symbolic coherence by communicating meaning independently with no need of a surrounding system to supplement its incompleteness but it is in turn haunted by its own lack of ideological purity in that a Gothic Cathedral is not in itself the geometrical shape of ascension, and a Magian astrological catalogue is not in itself the geometrical shape of a layout of conflict.[130] At best, one can deduce the tendency towards ascension *from* the sense object but the geometrical shape always retains its transcendent status towards the object as its determinate limitation. Crossing the threshold from a modern day airplane to the abstract geometrical bias of an ascending ray of progress would result not in a new object but rather in the meme itself. The deep meme would overcome ideological purity by unambiguously stating the ideology of progress which was only implicitly observable in objects as geometrically impure as computers, smartphones, trash cans, and suburban homes. Yet this achievement of ideological purity reveals the meme's own transcendent determinate limitation to be its removal from the underlying resource for which it is itself merely the geometrical metaphor. An ascending ray of progress is not in itself the somatic body of petroleum, just as an agrarian circle is not in itself the somatic body of barley, sheep, or wheat. But achieving the determinate limitation by crossing the threshold to the resource itself dissolves the meme as a geometrically-intelligible shape and instead results in a sheer presence of a body which lacks even the basic features of form.

The a priori transcendent determinate limitation posed from one layer to another is only one of the three possible modal instantiations of relative limitation. In addition, a given unit of meaning successfully disclosed within one of the five layers of meaning has a transcendental limitation which fixes its morphological conditions of coherence by forcing it to conform to the anonymous features which any unit of meaning whatsoever within that layer would have to embody in order to be meaningful. For example, mythic events have nearly unlimited potential for variation at the empirical level of content but every mythic event, insofar as it is a mythic event, is transcendentally limited by the requirements to be disclosed as a unified event rather than as a set of disconnected objects, characters, and props; by the requirement to be co-disclosed along with an implicit understanding of the central conflict against which the event strives to reach a resolution; and by the requirement to embody meaning through the ambiguous

---

[130] Spengler, Oswald. Decline of the West: Volumes 1 and 2 . Random Shack. Kindle Edition.

and poetically inconclusive horizon of a hermeneutical cycle of interpretation rather than a simple differentiation of one definite value from another. These are the a priori conditions of a mythic event, yet the mythic event's surface-level content does not directly embody them. They stand outside the content as the transcendental limitation which prefigures how the content will manifest itself. And yet they are also not transcendent to the mythic event as though they were some independent object like a cow in the field or even a separate layer outside of Mythology. The Hermeneutical Limitation, as the features which dictate mythic disclosure, make up the a priori transcendental limitation to its Being.

The other four layers each carry their own a priori transcendental limitation of manifestation with no common ground to the conditions of the mythic event. A systematic value is transcendentally limited by the requirements to be given as a value situated within a schema of rank relative to the full set of values and relative to the system as a whole. A value with identical surface level appearance but a different underlying system is a different value. The symbol "&" has no intrinsic or independent essence: within the C Programming Language, its meaning related to memory address is irreducible to its meaning as a logical "and" in a distinct linguistic or logical system. The transcendental limitation is the conditions which allow the value to appear.

Manifestation within the sense objective layer is bound by the transcendental limitation of the requirement to be disclosed as an independent entity rather than a value from a system, while the memological layer is bound by the transcendental limitation of the requirement to be given as an abstract geometrical shape rather than an object, and the Soma is bound by the transcendental limitation of the need to be given as a raw presence or absence with no further morphological or conceptual qualification.

By far the most mysterious of the relational modes of Limitation is the imminent limitation, in that it is the limitation which is intrinsically "within" the layer rather than located in some transcendent location beyond or as some transcendental filter providing the abstract conditions for manifestation. Yet the imminent limitation is the paradoxical notion of a limitation which is excluded from the content of a field despite the fact that it is still located somewhere on the inside; it is the bizarre notion of an inside outsider, or as an "extimate" remainder with no proper place in the very field to which it is still undeniably imminent.

The five transcendental registers of meaning vary at the level of a priori conditions of manifestation and at the level of minimal unit of meaning, but are bound by the common denominator of the substance which grounds all five of them in meaningfulness. In Aristotle's hierarchy of categories, substance holds a unique position because even if one is explicitly contemplating the object from the standpoint of one of the higher order categories, such as "place," one is still ultimately grasping the same substance even if one scales the ladder of categories to focus on its location.[131] Phenomenologically speaking, the substance is not somewhere outside the frame of meaning which happens to emphasize its location; rather, that frame is only meaningful insofar as it is really about the substance. The difference between the category of place and the category of substance per se is not so much a difference in content, in that in both cases the same substance is given: the difference is rather in which mode of meaning the same substance is manifested according to a different standard of value. Likewise, the memological, sense objective, systematic, and mythological layers are all manifestations of the same Soma through a standard of meaning denominated by the common standard of memological shape, objective form, systematic value, or mythological event rather than by the transcendental criteria of somatic presence per se.

Is the subject, however, just another substance which is also transitively carried over from one layer to another by virtue of being endowed with an overwhelming presence and undeniably real content? Or is the subject, rather, an excess which lingers from one layer to the next only because it cannot be transcendentally manifested by the criteria of any of the five layers? The subject is not in itself a mythological event that emerges into presence, unfolds over a set duration, and then fades out as another event

---

[131] Aristotle, *The Physics*, (New York: The Modern Library, 2002), p. 303.

replaces it on the stage of theatrical performance. Nor is the subject itself just a systematic value whose intelligibility results from its difference from the other values against which it is situated in a determinate schema of rank. Nor is the subject simply another sense object which manifests a worldview, the meaningfulness of which is contingent only upon its isomiorphism to the deep meme and somatic layers. Nor is the subject in itself a deep meme, insofar as even within our era one deep meme is fading out of being, to be replaced by another, yet the subject shall survive the coming and going of even the most seemingly-stable deep memes. Nor is the subject itself the Soma, for the Soma similarly can fade out of being but leave the subject behind to cope with this loss and rebuild over the ruins of meaning left in its default.

This peculiarity of the subject, that it cannot be fit into any particular manifest content but somehow survives the dissolution of even the most stable objective structures, has typically been treated by reversing the ontological standard of positivity to instead focus on the subject as a type of radical negativity. Slavoj Zizek's controversial work *The Ticklish Subject*, of course, broke expectations by actually *endorsing* Cartesianism in an era in which blaming Descartes on every problem from Colonialism to Capitalism to the Gender Inequality provided an easily-recyclable gimmick in the academic sophists' bag of tricks. Zizek did this by showing that the critiques of Descartes which repudiate the subject as a reified objective substance miss the entire point that what Descartes really discovered, and what Kant and Hegel later developed much more fully, was that the subject is not some positive entity with a fixed essence: rather, the subject is precisely the power of negativity which provides the raw potential for revolutionary political negations of problematic social orders to be carried out concretely.[132] In this book, Zizek demonstrated a particular liking for Hegel's "night of the world," in which monstrous apparitions like "a bloody head" and a "white ghastly apparition" demonstrate the subject's power of imagination is not a

---

[132] Zizek, Slavoj, *The Ticklish Subject* (London: Verso, 2000), p. 89.

synthetic reproduction of substantial data so much as it is the radical negation of any fixed content:

> [T]he power of imagination in its negative, disruptive, decomposing aspect [is best demonstrated by] the power that disperses continuous reality into a confused multitude of partial objects . . . Ultimately, imagination stands for the capacity of our mind to dismember what immediate perception put together.[133]

The implication, of course, is that the subject itself is simply this negativity. The primary danger of this overemphasis on negation is, of course, that it generates an unbounded optimism in the subject's ability to casually "negate away" any unjust but functional political or social structure in the guarantee that the resulting dissolution into negation was simply the subject's own ontological character reflected back into the medium of political objectivity. The author finds this to be deeply problematic as a general political principle, but fatal when transferred to the realm of Peak Oil. Peak Oil is not an illusory political essence which could be dialectically mediated away by the subject's negativity into some more advanced social form that would emerge through a dialectical progression of the "nothing negating itself." Peak Oil cannot be adequately handled from either the positive or negative ontological biases available thus far, insofar as even the subject who is called to act in response to Peak Oil is itself irreducible to either positive or negative categories. Yet the subject holds a bizarre stance towards limitation, in that subject is not only limited by the constraints of, say, Peak Oil. The subject quite literally is limitation.

In each layer of meaning, a certain set of elements will manifest themselves within the frame of intuition. In the mythological layer, an event will emerge, populated by characters, setting, props, and even an implicit conflict which provides the narratological context for the event. Yet if one were to collect every element in the frame of the event into a set, even if the set had

---

[133] Ibid., p. 30.

captured every one of them there would still be a remainder that had gone unaccounted for: the subject to whom the event appeared. Descending to the register of the System will not remove this limitation. If one were to collect all the symbolic elements of some formal system like Russell's *Principia Mathematica* or Euclid's *Elements*, there would still be one extant remainder that could not be integrated into the system because it was not a value that could be located in rank relative to the other values: this would be the subject to whom the system manifested itself. One would find the same in descending to the sense objective, memological, and somatic layers, for even the Soma's παρουσία (Parousia) would be meaningless without some subject to whom it would be disclosed as presence. Even the archaic, non-New Testament meaning of Parousia typically referred to the presence of some important person, like a king, but this presence would be meaningless if there were no one at all to whom it would be a presence. Likewise, the subject is the bizarre remainder which escapes enumeration by even the most sophisticated numerical system but escapes precisely because it is *not* located somewhere beyond the frame in which every other element was properly accounted for. The subject is almost like a ghost who cannot be grasped despite the fact that one's hands occupy exactly the same physical coordinates as the ghost but still only end up grabbing handfuls of empty air. The subject is not, however, an empty illusion which must be deconstructed away in order to restore rationality to a field which risks madness if left contaminated by such an irrational excess. The subject's existence can only be accounted for within the ontological horizon of limitation rather than either positivity or negativity, for the subject is just the imminent limitation which each frame of intuition embodies: the subject is the limit which remains after the total set of elements is subtracted from a field of manifestation but an excess still endures:

Haag's Theorem:

Imminent Limitation = Field of Intuition - {Set of All Accountable Elements}

Likewise, the tendency in Existentialism to conceptualize the subject's relation to limitation in negative terms must be revised. In *The Concept of Anxiety*, Kierkegaard described the object of anxiety as "nothing," insofar as the existentialist subject in its orientation towards death lacks any firm ground on which to secure a guarantee for personal action, leading the subject no choice except to have to make a groundless choice with a leap of faith.[134] The author would suggest that the subject is not "nothing" in a negative sense so much as the subject is the imminent limit to the field of intuition which manifests itself without ever incorporating the subject as one of the elements of the set of givens. The subject does not therefore relate to limitation as a dimensional limitation of a boundary so much as the subject is forced to relate to limitation as its own ontological characteristic. The subject *is* insofar as it is limitation. Yet the field of intuition given in consciousness enjoys a strange relationship with this limit in that the loss of the imminent limitation of subjectivity would not cleanse the field of givens from some alien content which had intruded upon its purity: rather, the field would vanish with the loss of its limit, because contents can only appear as phenomena if there is a subject to whom they appear. Limitation is a matter of Being in the sense that the loss of the limit is simultaneously the loss of existence, insofar as the field of positive givens was only sustained ontologically by the anomalous non-element of a limit which could neither be integrated positively nor excised negatively. The subject therefore sustains the Being of the field of consciousness through which intuition is given, through limitation.

Yet in addition to this subjective limitation, the field is sustained ontologically by the substantial limitation which the Soma provides, in that the disappearance of the Soma would simultaneously collapse the entire hierarchy of mythological, systematic, sense objective, and memological meanings which were built upon this foundation in a relation of limitation built on substance rather than subject.

---

[134] Kierkegaard, Soren, *The Concept of Anxiety* (Princeton: Princeton University Press, 1980), p. 61.

[1]

| Field | Transcendent Limit | Transcendental Limit | Imminent Limit |
|---|---|---|---|
| Somatic | Absolute Limitation | Presence | Existential Subject |
| Memological | Soma | Shape | Existential Subject |
| Sense Objective | Deep Meme | Form | Existential Subject |
| Systematic | Sense Object | Value | Existential Subject |
| Mythological | Systematic Value | Event | Existential Subject |

This table demonstrates that each layer "exists" only insofar as it is limited, yet this limitation is not a mysterious uniform abstraction, some vague notion about which one cannot say anything more specific than that it is "limitation." Rather, each layer only exists insofar as it bears the imminent limitation of a subject; the transcendent limitation of the foundation provided by a deeper layer (or in the case of the deepest layer, the foundation of Absolute Limitation); and the transcendental limitation of each layer's formal requirements of manifestation (as event, as value, as object, as shape, as presence.) In a certain sense, therefore, the manifestation is the ontic entity held together by the ontological structures of limitation but irreducible to any of them. Manifestation cannot be reduced to the subject (imminent limit), the substance (transcendent limit), or even the transcendental frame of meaning (transcendental limit) and yet, the removal of even one of the three would cause the manifested appearance to vanish into nothingness instantly. Without a subject for the appearance to appear to, there would be no appearance; similarly, without a substance to sustain the appearance in the firm ground of reality, there would be no appearance; finally, without some transcendental requirements dictating *how* the appearance is to appear, there would be no appearance.

This "manifestation" provides the sole positive ontic content in the midst of three origins of limitation, each vaguely related to Absolute Limitation as the possibility to cease existing. Many of even the great philosophers have mischaracterized the manifestation by equating it with one of its limitations rather than grasp the relation of limitation as such.

New Age solipsism promises the manifestation is nothing more than a product of spiritually-attuned consciousness, in which the subject can directly generate the appearance with his or her mind, since consciousness is thought of not as a limit but as an all-encompassing container in which all reality unfolds according to its whims.

Marxist Materialism made the same error in reverse by mischaracterizing the manifestation as the ideology, a false consciousness generated by the substance of the material modes of production; in this case, the substance was not conceived of as a limit but rather as a positive entity with a unique agency to produce ideologically-distorted consciousness as its side effect.

Finally, German Idealism mischaracterized the manifestation as the production of the transcendental form gone mad, as Kant's notion of a transcendentally-schematized form from the Imagination which is then subsumed under the concept in the Understanding to produce meaning was revolutionized in German Idealism to become a Notion which generates its own form and content through negating itself; appearance was just the "Picture Thinking' which distorted notional mediation into what appeared to be a fixed or static entity but which was in reality radically unfixed.

The question remains, however, what one should call this manifestation in light of its status as an entity which exists ontically only on condition that it remain limited. Earlier in the chapter dedicated to Soma, the author mentioned the following quote from Pseudo-Paul in 2 Thessalonians 2:8-9:

καὶ τότε ἀποκαλυφθήσεται ὁ ἄνομος

This quote is typically translated as something like "and then the Antichrist will be revealed" but its literal translation from the Greek is closer to "and then the lawless one will be apocalypsed." The Greek word ἀποκαλυφθήσεται should not be read as a catastrophic event that destroys the world; it should be read as the negation of a covering-over. The text warns that the lawless one will someday be uncovered into appearance: one could say that he will be "apocalypsed into manifestation, in line with the threefold relative limitation against the background of Absolute Limitation." Part 4 of the present work shall develop this thesis further by revealing that in our era, we are witnessing a crisis of apocalyptic character in that in our era the apocalypse is precisely that appearance is failing to properly be apocalypsed into manifestation. The five layers risk blending into one indeterminate, confused mess in which electronic states in machines are mistaken for Gnostic numbers; pre-programmed self-moving pixels on computer screens which choke out any need for hermeneutical involvement or subjective interpretation are mistaken for Mythology; counter sense machines which burn the Soma are mistaken, somehow, for the Soma itself such that "Technology will Save Us" from the negative effects of itself; and the memological bias of progress is mistaken for a "scientific truth" directly revealed from Nature rather than as the transcendental shape that allows revelation to take place at all. These confusions threaten to collapse the apocalypsed appearance into a dull echo of indifference. The apocalypse in our era is precisely that the apocalypse as a revelation of the appearance in line with its limitations is coming dangerously close to failing to happen.

*The Power Process and Imminent Limitation*

Because the subject quite literally is limitation, it would seem absurd to speak of "existentialist freedom" in the context of a subject whose very ontological makeup would seem to embody the contradiction of freedom, in that a limitation is traditionally conceived of as the primary obstacle to be overcome in order for freedom to become free. However, the author shall argue that in Ted Kaczynski's meditations on the Power Process, the most important intellectual work on freedom of our contemporary era, freedom cannot be understood except through an understanding of the subject as imminent limit.

In *Industrial Society and its Future*, Kaczynski defined the Power Process as a basic human need. Its four elements include: a goal; expended effort towards the goal; the achievement of the goal; and, preferably, freedom over how to go through the process. Kaczynski later provided a definition of freedom which included a reference to the Power Process as the context in which real freedom had to be actualized:

> By 'freedom,' we mean the opportunity to go through the Power Process, with real goals not the artificial goals of surrogate activities, and without interference, manipulation, or supervision from anyone, especially from any large organization.[135]

The primary problem Kaczynski identified with modernity and the rise of fossil fuel-based technology was that it totally deprived the individual of opportunities to go through the Power Process to fulfil serious survival needs such as hunting, gathering, or even growing one's own crops or raising goats. Instead, all basic survival needs were met through distributing industrial products over commercial networks in which one's obedience to the system was the *only* factor which would determine whether one got access to enough food, shelter, and clean water to survive.[136] This lack of opportunity to go through the Power Process to meet survival needs led to an explosion in what he called "surrogate activities," trivial activities which allow one to go through the Power Process just for the sake of getting to go through the Power Process. Activities as seemingly pointless as collecting stamps, cheering for one particular football team, or even doing Science were therefore revealed to just be outlets which the system tolerates in order to allow the subject to meet a basic psychological need without posing any danger to the technological system.

---

[135] Kaczynski, Ted, *Industrial Society and its Future*, in *Technological Slavery* (Port Townsend: Feral House, 2010), p. 64.
[136] Ibid., p. 49.

Kaczynski was careful to note, however, that even leftists, the most over-socialized of all people, were still prone to devote ridiculous amounts of energy to surrogate activities which merely addressed their frustrated need for power as the most obedient to the system of modern technology: political activism was revealed to be just one more surrogate activity with no essential teleological difference from something as innocuous as collecting coins.[137]

Kaczynski's insights into this need to go through the Power Process present something of an ontological riddle. If the subject is fundamentally positive in nature, he or she would have no need to go through the Power Process because he or she would already be complete; a stone, for example, has no such drive because it has no need to supplement an existentialist lack because its essence already fully overlaps with its existence. Yet, similarly, if the subject was fundamentally negative, he or she would be able to step over the limits of the Power Process by deconstructing it or negating it away and withering its solid foundations into so much dead matter to be swept away in the winds of dialectical progress. After all, much of Postmodernist and Marxist Philosophy has amounted to endless repetitions of the academically-fashionable cliché that the subject doesn't exist and that the illusion of Cartesian Dualism is the cause of all social injustice in the world. The coherent subject would therefore be devolved to just another static form which only appears to be fixed to the "Picture Thinker" who is too naïve to realize that the Notional Thinking of negative dissolution will soon submit this form to abstract negation. Neither the positive nor the negative characterization would allow us to grasp a subject with a fundamental need to go through the Power Process.

The only way to understand this, especially in the context of the technological system, is through an Ontology of Limitation. The subject is an excess which remains even after the most conclusive systematic attempt to integrate, analyse, and re-order the sum total of all extant values in a field. Even leftists, the subjects who willingly give themselves over to the system to be moulded into submissive parrots of its ideology, paradoxically manifest an even

---

[137] Ibid., p. 106.

*greater* need and even greater attachment to their surrogate activity of political activism. Even the subjects who appear to simply be "the system itself," such as presidents, CEOs, and dictators are themselves just subjects who linger in the system as an imminent limitation which can never be fully reduced to objective parts of the system. Kaczynski's later essay "The System's Neatest Trick" made clear that the system cannot be confused with the human subjects who appear to be in control of it:

> Let's begin by making clear what the System is not. The system is not George W. Bush and his advisors and appointees, it is not the cops who maltreat protesters, it is not the CEOs of the multinational corporations, and it is not the Frankensteins in their laboratories who criminally tinker with the genes of living beings. All of these people are servants to the System, but they themselves do not constitute the system.[138]

If the subject were just some positive content, it would be easily incorporated into the system, processed into some industrial result, neutralized into harmlessness, and then passed over. But the system can never succeed in fully de-subjectivizing the subject, since the subject is wedged deep into the system itself as its own imminent limit to existence. The mentat in *Dune* might similarly be considered to be the excess of subjectivity who refines the non-systematic skills of awareness and meditation on limitation rather than compete with machines at the gnostic game of systematic manipulation, yet this is precisely because the mentat is the limit to the system which can never be incorporated.[139] The Butlerian Jihad is in many ways the revelation that the subject can never be fully domesticated into systematicity; it can only be destroyed.

Our modern technological system is not an abstraction which floats indifferently to the phenomenological intuition in which it can be made manifest: the system is, rather, sustained in

---

[138] Kaczynski, Ted, "The System's Neatest Trick," in *Technological Slavery* (Port Townsend: Feral House, 2010), p. 193.
[139] Herbert, Frank, *Dune* (New York: Ace Books, 1990), p. 208.

existence solely by the substantial limit of the Soma of fossil fuels and by the imminent limit of the subject to whom it is made manifest. The subject's freedom is not therefore some positive energy which seeks to clear away limitation as an obstacle to its actualization; freedom is, rather, simply the conceptualization of what is inherently an imminent limit rather than a positive or even a negative entity.

### Revolution and Limitation

The genuine existentialist stance does not entertain fantasies of unlimited freedom to transform the material world to conform to some far-flung political revolutionary ideology. The caricature of existentialist freedom as an unbridled license to pursue selfish gain simply to "prove to the world" that the subject is absolutely free is a caricature deeply at odds with the content of the classical existentialist novels of Dostoyevsky. The murder committed in *Crime and Punishment* should not be read as a demonstration that the subject is so radically, groundlessly free from limitation that he was free enough to commit even a senseless, pointless criminal act just to prove that the limitation preventing him from doing so was illusory. Rather, the murder does not release the subject to actualize his radical negation of limits; it reveals that even after one arbitrary transcendent limitation had been overstepped, the subject's own relation to limitation was left completely unaffected. Dostoyevsky's paradox is: how does accomplishing a radical leap towards freedom actually make the subject even less free? The subject had misread his own ontological constitution as limitation as the external limit posed by an arbitrary obstacle, the removal of which did nothing to change his unclarified relation to his own essence.[140]

*Notes from the Underground* demonstrates the same paradox, in that the man who lives his life holed up in an apartment without ever doing anything is not unfree due to a lack of risky leaps into actions he was previously too afraid to do. Rather, the subject is made even *more* unfree in his reckless stabbings in the

---

[140] Dostoyevsky, Fyodor, *Crime and Punishment*, in *Fyodor Dostoyevsky: The Complete Novels (Centaur Classics)*, Kindle Edition.

dark at tasks he knew he was better off not trying. It would be hard to imagine that inviting oneself to a party to which one is not welcome with people one does not even like represents a "glorious overcoming of limits," even though at some level the narrator did manage to force himself into such a situation, despite the catastrophic results that inevitably followed from it. Even at the end, when the narrator invites the troubled prostitute Liza to his home, she honours his request with the best intentions of having a friendly and productive meeting but somehow the narrator is still unable to overcome his existential limitations to freedom, even in the moments in which he blindly tries the hardest to force an event into actuality which would be better left undone.[141] Sheer effort alone is clearly insufficient:

> It was not only that I could not become spiteful, I did not know how to become anything: neither spiteful nor kind, neither a rascal nor an honest man, neither a hero nor an insect.[142]

Lest anyone suggest that the narrator of *Notes from the Underground* is just one troubled person who cannot be read as a prototype for the existentialist predicament of the subject, Dostoyevsky was quite clear at the beginning of the text that narrator is basically "everyone" rather than one deranged individual. Even if one were to grant that that novella was Dostoyevsky's supreme literary exposition of the individual, his later novel *The Possessed* could be read as his greatest literary exposition of the community. In *The Possessed*, an entire community of intellectuals in Russia finds that same strained relation towards freedom and action, in that no amount of raw, deliberate, forced action can ever succeed in actually making any one of them free. The individuals in that novel do not suffer from a lack of risky or bold action: on the contrary, the novel is filled with murders and suicides that represent among the most deadly serious of all actions that still never make

---

[141] Dostoyevsky, Fyodor, *Notes from the Underground*, in *Three Short Novels of Dostroyevsky* (New York: Garden City Books, 1960), p. 295.
[142] Ibid., p. 181.

the subject any freer as a result. One character goes as far as to speculate whether committing suicide would provide the ultimate proof of God's non-existence, since if God does not exist the subject would be so free that he could even destroy himself.[143] In one sense, suicide blots out the imminent limitation of the subject; however, *no one* could rationally argue that that would actualize the freedom which proved so elusive in all of Dostoyevsky's classical works on the subject. *The Possessed* largely documents the community's attempt to appropriate radical Western European Political Philosophy in order to forcibly leap into the freedom which the "backward" conservative, Orthodox, traditional Russian context seemed to limit: they find instead that Nihilism is the only result.

The subject's existence is therefore not unfettered celebration of the unlimited power to negate any determinate positive content whatsoever and reorder the cosmos to actualize some abstract political fantasy. The subject's existence is, rather than an orgasmic absorption in unchecked freedom, just a terrible realization that the subject does not even have enough freedom to definitively overcome the anxiety of existence, as Kierkegaard goes on to note in *Fear and Trembling*:

[T]o exist as the single individual is the most terrible of all.[144]

Jordan Peterson's most important political insight, as something of an existentialist thinker himself, is that dabbling in political revolution is unjustifiably risky even in the cases where one appears to have bulletproof rational understanding of the corrupt structures one seeks to eliminate. In reality, we cannot actually fully understand *why* entrenched structures which have evolved over countless generations function; we only know that abruptly destroying them will result in something that *does not* function. Ironically enough, the destruction of traditional social

---

[143] Dostoyevsky, Fyodor, *The Possessed*, in *Fyodor Dostoyevsky: The Complete Novels (Centaur Classics)*, Kindle Edition.
[144] Kierkegaard, Soren, *Fear and Trembling* (Princeton: Princeton University Press, 1983), p. 75.

forms was not only not an expression of unrestricted freedom, it also failed to make the subject feel any freer afterwards:

> In many households in recent decades, the traditional household division of labour has been demolished, not least in the name of liberation and freedom. That demolition, however, has not left so much glorious lack of restriction in its wake as chaos, conflict and indeterminacy. The escape from tyranny is often followed not by paradise but by a sojourn in the desert, aimless, confused, and deprived.[145]

Above all, Peak Oil Philosophy must resist the temptation to adopt utopian fantasies that in the wake of Peak Oil, some pet political ideology will be favoured by the course of History to universally restructure society in accord with any one person's private biases, many of which are themselves far more dependent upon Fossil Fuels than that person realized. Gleefully awaiting the Revolution for its promise for "Social Progress" (a mere euphemism for the belief that in the future, everyone will think exactly the same on controversial political and religious issues) must serve as a sign that someone has missed the entire point of Peak Oil and may possibly serve as an indicator that that person cannot be taken seriously as a genuine member within the movement at all. Rather, Peak Oil will entail the courageous acceptance of sacrifice, hard work, a decreased standard of living, and a greater need to accept a flawed world where religious and political disagreement will not be overcome but will likely become even more pronounced. Rather than absolute freedom, Peak Oil will require the humility to accept that conditions cannot be magically negated away.

It will no doubt be controversial to suggest, but the author feels that several millennia of Christian Tradition may suddenly prove beneficial to consult, if not for religious reasons then at least for an insight into how pre-modern thinkers grappled with a flawed world before the introduction of Fossil Fuels convinced them that

---

[145] Peterson, Jordan, *12 Rules for Life* (New Delhi: Allen Lane, 2018), p. 271.

these flaws could just be erased through burning enough fossil fuels to force the world to approximate a "perfect state." Pre-Modern Christian views on the world as *fundamentally imperfect* did not tend to await a utopia that would materialize as a result of any particular political party or social change. Yet somehow, this spirit of resignation in the face of imperfection arguably generated a more productive attitude towards the hard labour and personal sacrifice that needed to be accepted to make a world without Fossil Fuels liveable. It is only when one conceivably believes that there is enough fossil fuel energy to force a universal, globalized change into effect overnight that one is rendered incapable of accepting even the slightest disagreement ideologically or the slightest imperfection in the social body. Volume Two of the present work will continue the discussion of Politics and Religion for Peak Oil Philosophy in much greater detail. In closing, the conditions of decline will instead provide the test of whether Finitude is taken seriously as a principle for one's life or not. The implications of finitude for Truth will be the subject of Part IV of the present volume.

# Part III
# Truth

"Felix quem Veritas per se ipsam docet, non per figuras et voces transeuntes, sed sicuti se habet." — Anonymous, *De Imitatione Christi*[146]

---

[146] "Happy is the man whom Truth by itself doth teach, not by figures and transient words, but as it is in itself."

# Chapter Five
# Apocalypsed Not:
# The Crisis of Manifestation in the Twilight of Fossil Fuels

*Heidegger, John of Patmos, and the Essence of Technology*

Part III of the present work concluded with a discussion of the proper terminology by which to speak about the ontic appearance which is sustained by the ontological grounding of the imminent limit of the subject, the transcendent limit of the Soma, the transcendental limit of a particular register of meaning, and the Absolute Limitation by which it could cease to exist at any time. Properly constituted, the appearance that emerged would be "apocalypsed" into manifestation, following the Koine Greek distinction in the New Testament manuscripts between Parousia (Presence) and Apocalypse (Revelation.) The chapter dedicated to Soma demonstrated that presence is *not* appearance, since Jesus' Second Presence would disclose the very horizon for an appearance to emerge. This was due to the difference in status between the Soma (in Paul's case, Jesus) as a transcendent limit and the appearance as an ontic entity. At any rate, the New Testament manuscripts do not suggest that Jesus' Second Presence would be bound by the Phenomenological requirements of achieving a coherent image displayed in the medium of sight, since Jesus' Second Presence would abruptly transform the world from a fallen world stained by sin into the world of the judgment day, in which damnation or redemption would set in for everyone all at once. Regardless of whether one accepts Parousia as a religious concept, the New Testament manuscripts at the very least demonstrate a philosophical concept of presence remarkably different from what Derrida and the other Postmodernist thinkers have rejected so vehemently. Primarily, the difference lies in the way that Parousia does not deal with images but rather with the somatic basis that allows an image to be disclosed within one of the five registers of meaning in the first place. The realm of images is, rather, Apocalypse.

It is worthwhile to briefly examine the Koine Greek New Testament references to Apocalypse to see how this concept differs from Parousia (Presence.) Of course, the final book in the canonical New Testament is dedicated to this theme, in that it is quite literally called "The Apocalypse (ἀποκάλυψις) of John the Divine." The opening words of the document also indicate that what follows will be an "Apocalypse of Jesus Christ" ("ἀποκάλυψις ἰησοῦ χριστοῦ"):

ἀποκάλυψις ἰησοῦ χριστοῦ, ἣν ἔδωκεν αὐτῷ ὁ θεός, δεῖξαι τοῖς δούλοις αὐτοῦ ἃ δεῖ γενέσθαι ἐν τάχει, καὶ ἐσήμανεν ἀποστείλας διὰ τοῦ ἀγγέλου αὐτοῦ τῷ δούλῳ αὐτοῦ ἰωάννῃ, ὃς ἐμαρτύρησεν τὸν λόγον τοῦ θεοῦ καὶ τὴν μαρτυρίαν ἰησοῦ χριστοῦ, ὅσα εἶδεν. μακάριος ὁ ἀναγινώσκων καὶ οἱ ἀκούοντες τοὺς λόγους τῆς προφητείας καὶ τηροῦντες τὰ ἐν αὐτῇ γεγραμμένα, ὁ γὰρ καιρὸς ἐγγύς.

The revelation from Jesus Christ, which God gave him to show his servants what must soon take place. He made it known by sending his angel to his servant John, who testifies to everything he saw—that is, the word of God and the testimony of Jesus Christ. Blessed is the one who reads aloud the words of this prophecy, and blessed are those who hear it and take to heart what is written in it, because the time is near.

A few things immediately stand out in stark contrast with Paul's meditations on the "Parousia of Jesus Christ." Jesus Second Presence is decidedly *not* a vision to be literally seen, because if it were nothing more then an image to be perceived than Jesus would have to physically travel from Jerusalem to Smyrna to Corinth to Rome and meet each believer individually to transform the old world into the new world one square meter of real estate at a time. Of course, Parousia has no intrinsic relation to vision. It is interesting to note, though, that the "Apocalypse of Jesus Christ" is explicitly portrayed as a vision which John of Patmos saw and which the believers will personally see when it repeats as a historical event accessible to the public. The opening lines state that the "time is near" for this repetition to take place. In that sense, the Apocalypse is a manifestation which will have occurred twice: once for John, once for each of the other Christians. The text of the Apocalypse is not itself the Apocalypse: it is only a linguistic warning to prepare the community of believers for the real thing, which will have to occur as a visually-witnessed event.

These references to visual intuition are not foreign to the text itself: John of Patmos explicitly states that he "testifies to everything *he saw*" (ἰωάννῃ, ὃς ἐμαρτύρησεν . . . . ὅσα εἶδεν.) The content of the Apocalypse, the visual correlate to John of Patmos' act of vision, is quite literally therefore the Idea (εἶδος, the same word Plato used to designate the Forms which the disembodied soul could see in an act of purified intuition, and the same basic concept which Descartes later used to describe Ideas as mental pictures which the cogito could view clearly and distinctly).[147]

Interestingly, Paul also speaks about "apocalypses of the Lord" ("ἀποκαλύψεις κυρίου") in the context of visions which an unnamed friend of his experienced when he was "caught up to . . . Third Heaven," but Paul laments that the content of this apocalypse was too sublime to translate into words. That is to say, the apocalypse of Jesus is so bound to the essence of a visual Idea that it is not even possible to isomorphically fit it into the symbolic material of language:

> ἐλεύσομαι δὲ εἰς ὀπτασίας καὶ ἀποκαλύψεις κυρίου. οἶδα ἄνθρωπον ἐν χριστῷ πρὸ ἐτῶν δεκατεσσάρων _ εἴτε ἐν σώματι οὐκ οἶδα, εἴτε ἐκτὸς τοῦ σώματος οὐκ οἶδα, ὁ θεὸς οἶδεν _ ἁρπαγέντα τὸν τοιοῦτον ἕως τρίτου οὐρανοῦ. καὶ οἶδα τὸν τοιοῦτον ἄνθρωπον _ εἴτε ἐν σώματι εἴτε χωρὶς τοῦ σώματος οὐκ οἶδα, ὁ θεὸς οἶδεν ὅτι ἡρπάγη εἰς τὸν παράδεισον καὶ ἤκουσεν ἄρρητα ῥήματα ἃ οὐκ ἐξὸν ἀνθρώπῳ λαλῆσαι. ὑπὲρ τοῦ τοιούτου καυχήσομαι

> I will go on to visions and revelations from the Lord. I know a man in Christ who fourteen years ago was caught

---

[147] Descartes, Rene, *Meditations*, in *The Rationalists* (New York: Anchor Books, 1974), p. 142.

up to the third heaven. Whether it was in the body or out of the body I do not know—God knows. And I know that this man—whether in the body or apart from the body I do not know, but God knows—was caught up to paradise and heard inexpressible things, things that no one is permitted to tell.[148]

John of Patmos, however, has no difficulty finding the words to communicate his own apocalypse to the community of believers, and in fact the bizarre images of his text have captivated Christians for millennia: the dragon, the Whore of Babylon, the lamb with seven horns and seven eyes, the Beast from the Sea, and the Beast from the Earth are only some of the more memorable images apocalypsed into manifestation in his *Revelation*.

Although John of Patmos' Apocalypse was the only one to be accepted into the canon, there were numerous apocalypses in Ancient Christianity. In fact, there are three known texts claiming to be the "Apocalypse of Peter" alone. The *Apocalypse of Peter* found in the Egyptian monk's tomb in which the *Gospel of Peter* was discovered at the end of the nineteenth century provides one of the best examples of the genre. Nearly a millennium before Dante, this text provides a tour of Hell, complete with a catalogue of punishments suited to particular kinds of sins. Jesus himself reveals this apocalypse to Peter in order that it might be written down as a warning for the public for the Judgment Day. The text quite literally states that Jesus' apocalypse revealing Hell was an "image of that which shall be accomplished at the last day" and that this apocalypse was inscribed on Jesus' "right hand," a very clear testament to its character as a literal appearance to be viewed.[149] The images which follow are quite graphic and are indisputably meant to be seen rather than just vaguely felt. For example, we learn that the souls of innocent people who were murdered will be personally escorted to Hell to view their murderers' eternal punishment from a safe distance:

---

[148] 2 Corinthians 12:1-5
[149] Anonymous, *The Apocalypse of Peter*, in *Lost Scriptures: Books that did not Make it into the New Testament* (Oxford: Oxford University Press, 2003), p. 282.

> [T]he angel Ezrael shall bring forth the souls of those who have been slain, and they shall behold the torment of those who slew them and say to one another, 'Righteousness is the judgment of God.'[150]

Later, we find that the greedy shall be "clad in rags and filthy garments" and that usurers will be up to their knees in filth.[151] We even learn that "servants who were not obedient to their masters" will be found "gnawing their tongues without ceasing."[152]

Regardless of the religious question of whether they are "really true" or not, these references to Apocalypse display a marked difference from the general concept of Parousia as a presence unique to the Soma. The apocalypse is undoubtedly the achievement of a coherent appearance within one of the five registers, sustained by the imminent subject, transcendent substance, and transcendental conditions. Because apocalypse only exists insofar as it is literally limited by subject, substance, and transcendental condition, apocalypse is a dependent rather than independent content. Likewise, it is not unique to any one particular layer of meaning. A disclosed narratological event is a mythological apocalypse. A successfully calculated mathematical result is a gnostic apocalypse. A tool which succeeds in "making sense" in an ergonic context of work is a sense objective apocalypse.[153] A deep meme which successfully structures consciousness is a memological apocalypse. Apocalypse is not some firm substance preceding its manifestation, so much as the apocalypse is simply the manifestation as it is given. But because it has no permanent endurance or ontological integrity outside of the structures of limitation which allow it to come to light, there is no guarantee that

---

[150] Ibid., p. 284.
[151] Ibid.
[152] Ibid., p. 285.

[153] From ἔργον, the Greek word for "work." Volume Two shall discuss ergonic contexts much more fully in the practical contexts of Ethics, Politics, and Religion.

the apocalypse will be achieved and that appearance will shine forth into unconcealment, as Heidegger is fond of putting it.[154]

As was mentioned earlier in the present volume, Heidegger himself realized this much, for his argument in "The Question Concerning Technology" is that Modern Technology is not the literal set of machines upon which either messianic hopes or demonic fears might be projected by individuals on the basis of their own subjective biases. Rather, Heidegger showed that the Essence of Modern Technology is in itself nothing technological, because Modern Technology is above all a change in the way that appearances are revealed. The Ancient Greek notion of Techne simply stated that whereas something brought to appearance by Nature (φύσις) emerged from its own natural principle of motion (such as a flower blooming from a plant), something brought to appearance by the skilled intervention of a craftsperson (such as pottery) was brought to appearance by Art rather than by Nature. This coming to appearance was Techne (τέχνη).

Heidegger recognized that the crisis of Modern Technology was that coming to appearance had devolved into a matter of treating everything, even including Man himself, as just so much raw material to be stockpiled into the "Standing Reserve" and stored for an industrial use to which it could be summoned at any moment. The predictable Derridean path might be to think of the Standing Reserve as the ultimate fulfilled intuition of excessive presence, since even the existentialist human subject would be reduced to a static object with no subjective agency in this arrangement. However, Heidegger argues that the exact opposite is the case: the problem in Modern Technology is that the Enframing through which it brings things to appearance as Standing Reserve is a kind of revelation that risks throwing "coming into appearance" as such into crisis :

> Enframing blocks the shining-forth and holding-sway of truth . . . Enframing threatens man with the possibility that it could be denied to him to enter into a more original

---

[154] Heidegger, Martin, "The Origin of the Work of Art" in *Poetry, Language, Thought* (New York: Harper Perennial, 1971), p. 74.

revealing and hence to experience the call of a more primal truth.[155]

The primary danger therefore is that the kind of quasi-revelation entailed by Modern Technology is a threat against revelation itself; the very horizon for Truth to occur as a happening risks collapsing in a de-worlded world in which unconcealement itself is blocked out:

> Enframing not only conceals a former way of revealing, bringing-forth, but it conceals revealing itself and with it that wherein unconcealment, i.e., truth, comes to pass.[156]

The author fully agrees with Heidegger's warnings about Modern Technology's threat to the very hermeneutical place in which Truth can happen as an event; however, the author will devote the remainder of the present volume to situating these claims within the context of an Ontology of Limitation to which Heidegger, operating with the Ontology of Dasein, did not have explicit access.

## *The Crisis of Limitation*

A crisis of limitation in our era is bringing about a strange reversal, in which the true apocalypse (in the colloquial sense of the term) is that the apocalypse (in the Koine Greek sense of the term) is running into danger of *not* happening. We are beginning to witness the end of manifestation and the death of appearance as such. If this is allowed to continue unchecked, it will mean the death of each of us as existential subjects, if not as physical persons as well.

The most surprising thing about the coming "apocalypse of the apocalypse" is that it is a crisis of limitation, but not in the sense one would expect. Typically, one would think that a crisis of

---

[155] Heidegger, Martin, "The Question Concerning Technology," In *The Question Concerning Technology and Other Essays* (New York: HarperColophon, 1977), p. 28.
[156] Ibid., p. 27.

limitation would posit the limit as a positive obstacle to be overstepped; the previous discussion of the Ontology of Limitation demonstrated, however, that Limitation is the only thing that sustains a positive ontic entity in its existence by providing the four limits (imminent, transcendent, transcendental, absolute) which cannot be absorbed into the appearance but provide its ontological support for being. Each of these limits which sustain the apocalypse qua manifestation is falling into crisis as the author writes these words. The transcendent limit of the Soma is obviously being burned out of existence through the unfolding historical problem of Peak Oil, as the entire volume of the present text has argued at length.

In addition, the imminent limit of the existential subject is falling into crisis, as excessive technological intermediation is beginning to break the subject's mentatic awareness and ability to penetrate to transcendent essences and objective truths. The subject is being reduced to a passive reflection of a set of pre-programmed illusions which pixelate on computer and smartphone screens at the request of an impersonal algorithm executed by a set of machines, the operations of which are not transparent even to the companies that own them. The algorithms themselves are not even unfolding "in consciousness" as the kind of authentic gnostic explorations of mathematical truth which Euclid, Archimedes, or Descartes once performed. Rather, these algorithms unfold as a gigantic pseudo-event that occurs to no one in particular, as the machines which execute them through burning electrical energy have no consciousness and reveal nothing directly to anyone's consciousness.

Even for the user with no interest in the internal workings of these machines, the subject is currently in danger of fading out of existence. Yet this is occurring precisely as a result of being absorbed in electronic screens which provide a pseudo-intuition which is so overwhelmingly filled-out that even the imminent limitation of a subject is in danger of being squeezed out of its privileged position as the "extimate limit which cannot be included in the set of positive contents of the field of intuition." The moment is soon arriving when mentatic subjects become as rare as free-will men at the end of George Orwell's 1984:

> If you are a man, Winston, you are the last man. Your kind is extinct.[157]

We have been driven so deep into the Cave that very few of us have any appreciation for the extent to which experiencing perceptions of a real world (let alone handling tools to build a woodworking project or feeding domesticated animals from which eggs and milk will be gathered) could be any different from watching a YouTube about the "same thing." One of the most interesting things Ted Kaczynski noted about spending years living in the wilderness as a hunter gatherer was that his senses were actually refined to a previously-unimaginable degree:

> The more intimate you become with Nature, the more you appreciate its beauty . . . [W]hen you live in the woods, rather than just visiting them, the beauty becomes a part of your life rather than something you just look at from the outside. [P]art of the intimacy with nature that you acquire is the sharpening of your senses. . . In the city life you tend to be turned inward, in a way. Your environment is crowded with irrelevant sights and sounds, and you get conditioned to block most of them out of your consciousness. In the woods you get so that your awareness is turned outward, toward your environment, hence you get more conscious of what goes on around you. For example, you'll notice inconspicuous things on the ground, such as edible plants or animal tracks. If a human being has passed through and left even just a small part of a footprint, you'll notice it. You know what the sounds are that come to your ears: This is a birdcall, that is the buzzing of a horsefly, this is a startled deer running off, this is the thump of a pine cone that has been cut down by a squirrel and has landed on a log.[158]

---

[157] Orwell, George, *1984* (New York: New American Library, 1977).
[158] Kaczynski, Ted, "An Interview with Ted" in *Technological Slavery* (Port

This proves, of course, that spending one's entire life staring at electronic screens, idling a car in heavy traffic, or sitting in an air conditioned office in a meeting with other prisoners of the Cave actually dull one's senses down to a state of near-uselessness. If pushed far enough, this will drive the subject out of its position of imminent limitation by risking to absorb it fully into the pixelated illusion and droning electronic noise which have no need for the subject to carry on; in fact, a disturbingly high number of people in recent years have squandered their final moments in front of a television set which continued running the same program even after the viewer had literally dropped dead in front of it. This situation has become immeasurably worse even since Kaczynski's era, in that he lived in urban areas of Illinois, Massachusetts, and California before the Internet and smartphones had become universal, constant, ubiquitous parasites on our attention and awareness. At that time, these city spaces were actually relatively non-technological compared to the environments of our era that are completely saturated with devices that are only one step away from dissolving the subject out of its position of imminent limitation.

      Finally, the transcendental limitations which distinguish one register of meaning from another by providing the abstract requirements of manifestation for each layer are in danger of being blotted out by the tendency for modern technology to replace authentically disclosed Phenomenological horizons of meaning with the confused, jumbled, a-regional, self-contradictory pixel illusions which are summoned to pseudo-appearance at the command of vast algorithms which are themselves self-contradictory affronts against the hierarchy of meanings. Both the pixel illusion and the technological origin that summons it to appear on one's smartphone screen are of an inherently ambiguous essence; they cannot be located within any one register in particular because they are a threat to the very ability for an appearance to be apocalypsed into manifestation. Aristotle's belief that essence was just another word for the object's form as given to properly-attuned intuition may

---

Townsend: Feral House, 2010), p. 405.

have finally found a conclusive counter-example, given that the pixel illusions on smartphone screens *do not* offer a window of essential insight by which a formal essence can be isolated in its morphological specificity.

The machine is increasingly not even the thing that is disclosed to us within the dimming horizon of pseudo-appearance. What we *don't see* pixelate on our smartphone screens is the physical piece of hardware (let alone the hundreds of thousands of them) located in some remote server farm, which executes an encrypted piece of software protected by corporate patents in a process accomplished by burning mountains of fossil fuel energy, a process which of course generates outright immoral levels of toxic pollution. Few people are aware that even an activity as seemingly-innocuous as sending emails regularly generates as much carbon dioxide pollution as driving a car. Further, nearly half of all data centre power consumption just goes to cooling hardware which would literally catch fire if left to natural processes. The 24/7 circus of internet consumption literally can only continue by wilfully putting out fires on a constant basis. But all of this is hidden from manifestation. There is no apocalypsed appearance by which these things can be understood even for the small handful of heretics foolhardy enough to venture into such supremely forbidden territory. Increasingly, the truth can only be reconstructed artificially from a conscious effort to reassemble a set of puzzle pieces from an incomplete set, one which massively-powerful corporate interests are intent on making sure one never finds the missing links to.

This lack of apocalypse cannot be dismissed as the result of not being allowed entry into some remote data centre, such that a simple act of visual perception into the building would wake up the world to its own insanity. The scariest thing is that we increasingly don't even "see" the physical device in our hands. The device as counter sense object vanishes from intuition as soon as some mind-numbing video clip begins playing or one's social media newsfeed kicks into gear to waste what little free time one has left in a day. It is not just that the contradictions of Modern Technology are clearly manifested in the counter sense object but tolerated only after a conscious act of hypocrisy: the contradictions themselves have become invisible, buried behind a pixel screen illusion which chokes out even one's ability to judge.

One might be tempted to think of Modern Technology as just an excessive Mythology that cancels out subjective interpretation and human imagination by overflowing the subject's awareness with the "ultimate mythological illusion" of self-moving pixels which play out a pre-programmed sequence of actions that leave no room for the subject to exist. Yet the pixels that materialize on the screen are themselves just the end result of a process conducted over the scope of the entire globe, involving billions of pieces of hardware. In fact, it is precisely the abstraction that Modern Technology is "just the device in your hand" that has fuelled the most counter-productive assumptions about it: the myth that the Internet is "free" or that it only costs as much as one's monthly cell phone bill has generated a reckless attitude of indifference and ignorance of the fact that, as John Michael Greer noted, the Internet is arguably the most energy-expensive piece of infrastructure ever built in human history. The pixel illusion is therefore *not* just a successfully disclosed mythological event. It is something which threatens the existence of Mythology altogether.

A machine located in some remote data centre is the "agent" that causes a certain content to appear on a smartphone screen many miles away, yet a piece of hardware stacked in a data centre is not given as a counter sense object because it is not disclosed to manifestation *as* a machine or even as an object of any kind. It is rather an invisible agent that operates as though by magic from an impossibly vast distance in a secret location to which the ordinary subject could never have access. One has lost even the ability to recognize a counter sense object as a counter sense object because it has been removed from the horizon of meaning.

On the other hand, the machine itself is just the physical instrument by which some vast algorithm filled with billions of symbols executes a task with an abstract uniformity that blots out the individuality of any particular device. Google is not "in" any one person's smartphone or laptop, nor even "in" any piece of hardware in any one particular data centre. Yet consulting its services from the privacy of one's own home does not "apocalypse" it to appearance as a gnostic essence within the systematic register of meaning either. The great traditional gnostic systems of the past allowed the subject to Phenomenologically penetrate into a transcendent gnostic essence, such as π or the square root of -1, as a result of carefully following a systematic pathway opened up within an authentic disclosure of the systematic register of meaning.[159] Euclid's *Elements* provided a thinker with a vast territory of exploration within the systematic register of meaning by "apocalypsing" ever more complicated results from the basis of carefully working from definitions and axioms, just as Muḥammad ibn Mūsā al-Khwārizmī's Medieval Persian treatise *The Compendious Book on Calculation by Completion and Balancing* provided an entryway into its own gnostic territory of exploration in the field of Algebra. But the Google Algorithm does not open up a gnostic space for the subject to explore. The difference is that Euclid's *Elements* does not just spit out results from a remote origin so obfuscated as to appear mystical; but Google *does* simply materialize the results in an instant from out of an abstract vacuum radically empty of any subjective penetration. Not only is the subject not given the thread to trace his or her path through the gnostic labyrinth; the subject is not even allowed entry.

    Modern Technology also cannot be located in the systematic register because, in many ways, one is not actually dealing with a gnostic system of abstractions. The paradox about these algorithms is that behind the façade of being ultra-rationalized, mathematically-formalized number-crunching schemas, in reality there is nothing rational about them. The essence of the algorithm is *thoroughly* empirical and only plagiarizes the resources of a priori rationality indirectly by pairing empirical expenditures of electricity with

---

[159] This is why Descartes' manifesto on Rationalist Philosophy *The Discourse on Method* emphasized that because every cogito is equally endowed with Reason, varying levels of access to truth depend not on whether one intrinsically has Reason but on which methodological pathway one pursues in order to work one's way through a revealed system of truths.
Descartes, Rene, *Discourse on Method*, in *The Rationalists* (New York: Anchor Books, 1974), p. 40.

pseudo-mathematical laws on an ad hoc one to one basis. Modern Technology does not literally store numbers, as though the Platonic Idea of a "3" or a "7" could be kidnapped and held hostage within a piece of hardware and then patented by some corporate asshole as his own "intellectual property." Paradoxically, there is not a single number in this monstrosity. There are only pseudo-numerical representations of numbers but these are electronic states that pseudo-isomorphically map high voltage and low voltage states to a contrived roster of pseudo-values, all of which ultimately decompose to binary pseudo-numerical signatures.

The grand irony is that amidst billions of algorithmic symbols, not a single number can be found. The algorithm does not open up a window of a priori truth in which the diligent subject can invest the hard labour to derive the geometrical truths of Euclid's *Elements* or the logical truths of Bertrand Russell's *Principia Mathematica*. There is no rational horizon of a priori validity there at all: this pseudo-system is *completely empirical*. The only literal truths about it include statements like "The machine is in a state of execution at this moment," "This section of hardware is in a high-voltage state," or "This section of hardware is in a low-voltage state."

This traditional distinction between rational and empirical contents must be examined a bit further before proceeding, as the author's argument for Truth hinges upon this distinction. In the Renaissance era of Modern Philosophy, abstract eternal truths that were not gained from experience were considered rational truths, as opposed to the empirical truths about contingent states of affairs gained from experience. For example, that four is the sum of two and two is a rational truth; this was not gained from experience because its contents (the numbers "4" and "2") are non-empirical. A "2" is not a physical object which can be seen (such as a cow in a field) because it is an abstract object with no physical existence. The subject can still access this truth only because it possesses Reason. On the other hand, a truth like "Delhi is located in Northern India" is an empirical truth. This is because the object of the truth is a physical object which could have just easily not existed at all or not existed in the way that it does. There was a time in the vastly distant past when Delhi did not exist because it had not yet been established as a human settlement. Yet even if we can grant that Delhi does exist, the subject who knows this only found out through experience: either by visiting the city himself or herself or by being notified of its existence by others.

Contrary to expectation, rational truths actually are more democratic than empirical truths. Descartes's argument defending Rationalist Philosophy on ethical grounds was precisely that:

> [R]eason is by nature equal in all men . . . the diversity of opinions, consequently, does not arise from some being endowed with a larger share of reason than others, but solely from this, that we conduct our thoughts along different ways, and do not fix our attention on the same objects.[160]

Truths such as the first 100 digits of $\pi$ may be intrinsically difficult to obtain, especially in the absence of modern computers, but they still *can* be obtained by an individual or group armed with nothing more than their own inherent Reason. In fact, the first 100 digits of $\pi$ were successfully unearthed in the 18$^{th}$ Century, long before any fossil fuel burning machines could be enlisted for aid.

Empirical truths only seem more democratic in contexts in which there is no explicit restriction to their access; however, empirical truths which are intentionally hoarded by powerful organizations under the guise of "intellectual property" are inherently undemocratic. There is no a priori pathway by which even the most gifted of Ancient or Medieval rational thinkers such as Pythagoras or Omar Khayyam could deduce the inner workings of Facebook with the use of their intellects alone. This is *certainly* not due to a lack of Mathematical giftedness; rather, it is due to the fact that Facebook does not actually traffic in anything mathematical. The *only* contents with which it deals are electronic states temporarily sustained by burning unspeakably huge amounts of fossil fuels in order to generate a profit (though of course, these companies are far less profitable than they may appear to be, as

---

[160] Descartes, Rene, *Discourse on Method*, in *The Rationalists* (New York: Anchor Books, 1974), p. 39.

Twitter has never turned a profit even once.) One cannot cheat around this fact by claiming that the scientific laws about electronic states provide a fully rationalized system which could be achieved by anyone with a functional mind. Rationalized laws about electronic states are not, themselves, the electronic states. Observing that a machine is in a state of execution at a given moment has no properly rational component: it is purely empirical.

One might object that a layer of terminological abstraction is draped over these expenditures of electrical energy, but even this layer is not a faithful window into the *a priori* realm of abstract Mathematics: it is just a sealed vault filled with arbitrary jargon invented out of whole cloth by a group of executives and other corporate parasites upon the Soma of Fossil Fuels. Wading through this fiercely-guarded swamp of artificial terms will not lead one to penetrate to the transcendent gnostic essence of any eternal truth. One will only find an industrially-marketed product rather than an objective essence, and an engineered invention rather than a Platonic Idea. Having a vast knowledge about C++ only displays that one was initiated into a corporate entity that provided this knowledge on empirical grounds alone; this knowledge was never deduced on rational grounds by Euclid or Muḥammad ibn Mūsā al-Khwārizm because it was not even something that could have been "true" in their eras. It is arguably not even "true" today except as a secondary euphemism for the simple empirical fact that an enormous amount of electricity is currently being burned by machines. In the far future when the machines are no longer running, it would be hard to imagine that all of this knowledge could be anything except false.

If one were to somehow teleport Archimedes into the United States today, he would never be able to deduce terms like "struct member," "List Comprehension," "Multiple Inheritance," or "Standard Library," with the resources of his intellect alone. This is not because of any deficiency on his part as a thinker. It is, rather, because these things *do not actually exist except as aliases for purely empirical expenditures of electrical energy.* They are nothing more and nothing less than the fossil fuel energy which they burn out of existence. The question of whether any of them is true today and whether they will be true in the far future when they will not even be capable of being "run" on any machine will be resumed later in the present chapter.

At any rate, Modern Technology has no proper place within the five transcendental registers of meaning. It fails to manifest itself as a pixelated mythology, as a sense object machine, or as a gnostic system of values because in reality it is none of these. More precisely, it disrupts each transcendental register of meaning and in turn breaks down the horizon of manifestation for each. One could go further and argue that Modern Technology is not a gnostic system because each value within it is only an empirical act of execution: a pseudo-value within a system only "exists" if the machine is plugged into a power source and is "running" that value in one form or another as a result. This is why behind the façade of "invincibility," the Cloud is one of the most fragile stores of information ever devised. A very short period of sustained worldwide electricity loss will be sufficient to lose all of the data stored there. This is because the data are not abstract values which could be rationally recovered through using the intellect to faithfully follow a rigorous mathematical procedure— they are just empirical expenditures of electrical energy that are temporarily stored in physical pieces of hardware but bear only the most fleeting and ephemeral kind of existence as a result.

However, making the leap of claiming that Modern Technology simply *is* the Soma of Fossil Fuels is the most horrifically incorrect stance of all. Modern Technology is not the Soma— it is only a tiny parasite which has temporarily hijacked its power. In our intuition that a CEO or company in the industry has a sublime amount of power, there is only a confused misrecognition that the Soma's sublime energy has temporarily been taken hostage by a few tiny, insignificant parasites who have misdirected the Earth's remaining fossil fuel energy resources to be wasted on trivial mind-numbing "entertainment" and on the unethical automation of jobs out of existence.

In the process, the Earth is progressively becoming more *unliveable* for future generations who will probably not be sympathetic to our generation's excuses for why their water sources were left undrinkable, their topsoil was reduced to desert, and their viable settlements were restricted to pockets of the globe not contaminated by industrial waste, virginal areas which will likely become rare enough to motivate horrific violent struggle in the not so distant future. Only the most delusional pseudo-subject of modernity could be fooled into thinking that sharing pictures of chalupas, drooling to hours of crass video entertainment, or trolling strangers on social media into committing suicide will be accepted as valid excuses for why the Earth was left in such terrible condition. Worse still, each of these activities only provided a few flickering moments of pseudo-satisfaction to the social media junkie who was left incapable of feeling a dopamine rush without a smartphone in his or her hand. We are literally destroying the Earth, and each other, for a few seconds of giggles. In the far future after the oil is gone and the machines are permanently turned off, those with enough remaining mentatic awareness to reflect on the situation may well ask themselves, was it worth it just for the lols?

## *The End of Ethics*

Any sane person should ask what state humanity has devolved down to if trolling strangers to death while sitting in one's underwear covered in Cheeto crumbs in front of a laptop screen at two in the morning just to avoid boredom could pass anyone's standard of Ethics. This is not even necessarily a matter of morality, although this image certainly is morally objectionable on many levels. Even in the absence of the modern notion of morality, one could consider this image to be an utter failure on the standard of Ancient Greek pagan Ethics. Aristotle's and Plato's views on Ethics were not that it was a list of prohibitions that forbade certain acts as sinful on arbitrary religious grounds which had to be dogmatically accepted through a renunciation of one's freedom (the modern secularist caricature of Ethics.) Rather, Plato and Aristotle were just interested in the question of what features set a good human being apart from a bad human being in the same way that a certain set of features set a good knife apart from a bad knife. Just as a good knife should be sharp enough to cut and made with a form that is safe and comfortable to handle, Aristotle listed the virtues a good human being should embody, such as courage, temperance, truthfulness, and ambition.[161] Each virtue did not simply have one vice as its opposite: rather, a virtue was the mean between two extremes, each of which was the vice against which the virtue was measured.

In Aristotle's era, the major ethical problem was, "How can one be a good human being?" In our era the major ethical problem is quickly becoming, "How can one be a human being at all?" We are in danger not only of losing good humans, but of losing humans altogether. The stereotypical story of a completely unlikeable individual who becomes a billionaire CEO in the technology industry despite being despised even by his own shareholders and employees who dread every moment they have to spend in his presence is often portrayed as proof that Modern Technology is paving the way for a utopia. The argument is apparently that computers are inherently democratic, in that a machine makes no judgments about an individuals' lack of manners or tact and will execute a literally-interpreted command regardless of *who* has requested it to be done. Likewise, rude and selfish behaviour that would have been socially inappropriate in contexts where one required minimal cooperation from other humans to survive would suddenly become a benefit: the further one pushed the limits of a machine for one's own narrowly-focused self-interest, the more successfully one would be able to outcompete others who were doing the same thing.

One fantasy for the near future is that soon every task in life will be similarly outsourced to the machines who will "level the field" by providing instantaneous services to anyone who demands them, no questions asked. As soon as even the vaguest desire emerges, the pseudo-subject will immediately click the appropriate button to meet this need. Hungry? Just click a button and robots will deliver processed junk food to your living space, no questions asked. Bored? Just click a button and enough videos (even including snuff films) to literally pass away the rest of your life in a state of drooling idleness will emerge. Frustrated and angry at no

---

[161] The complete list of virtues is a bit longer, of course. Aristotle, *Nicomachean Ethics* in *Basic Works of Aristotle* (New York: The Modern Library, 2002), p. 930.

one in particular? Just join the lynch mob of social media users who are flocking to the profile of the latest person caught saying something stupid. Horny? A sex robot with customizable features will be dispatched to your living space. Depressed? Don't worry, the euthanasia robots are on their way . . .

Even the most Soma-conscious Peak Oil thinker who realizes that the energy resources to create such a future for more than an extremely short period are not available should still seriously consider what this utopia would look like even if it were somehow able to materialize. Does the image of having 7 billion individuals trapped behind laptop screens impulsively jabbing at buttons as soon as the vaguest emotion stirs really sound like a utopia to anyone except the companies who hope to profit from this arrangement? Yet even they have failed to consider that even if an individual had an array of buttons lying before him or her, ready to meet any particular desire he or she might feel, that person would still need a minimally-functional hermeneutical horizon in which to evaluate even his or her own emotions coherently in order to know which button to click. Because of their implicit Positivist Metaphysical bias, the fools who promote this nonsense as utopia assume that a subject's emotions are fully transparent to himself or herself because an emotion would just need to travel within the closed circuit from body to mind, two positive pieces within a coherent whole. What they have failed to consider is that the subject's role as imminent limitation that sustains the disclosed Apocalypse is not a positive object included among the elements of the appearance; the subject is the limit whose escape from the appearance is precisely what allows it to emerge. In this "utopian future," however, both the Apocalypse-as-manifestation and its subjective limitation will be so thoroughly distorted that they will vanish. There may be a semi-conscious bundle of biological tissues propped up in front of the laptop screen, but it will not be a subject and it certainly will not be able to make rational judgments about how to use the buttons given to it. It is likely that the euthanasia robots will quickly become the most frequently requested service, as a vague and incomprehensible sense of purposelessness and hopelessness will set in but will lack even the horizon of meaning to be given as Angst!

Our current situation is actually not too far from this scenario. Already the vast majority of people's time is wasted staring at electronic screens which provide a gateway to services which promise to artificially meet nearly any desire on a moment's notice (at least to the extent that pixels on a screen and pre-recorded noises can meet such needs.) Yet rather than bring about universal happiness, an insurmountable sense of frustration, boredom, and dread characterize our era to an extent that truly was unthinkable in agrarian and hunter gatherer times: although Ted Kaczynski is highly critical of the politically correct myth that hunter gatherers held easy lives free of hard labour or social conflict, he does emphasize that many of the psychological ailments taken for granted in Modern Industrialism were unknown to hunter gatherers, since it is the technology itself that has caused them.[162] This is largely because the Apocalypse as manifestation is already collapsing out of existence and taking the subject along with it.

### *Is There Anybody Out There?*

It would be interesting to speculate how such a fantasy would be evaluated by the residents of the far future whose thinking will be structured by the Soma of post-industrial urban farming and the deep meme of the bell curve (while the linear ray is the deep meme of Oil, the bell curve literally is the deep meme of *Peak* Oil.) One could imagine visiting a community of goat herders in what remains of Northern California in the year 2200. Goats graze on weeds that have overrun the once-prosperous campuses in the Bay Area that have not been reclaimed by the Pacific Ocean. In the town nearby, the sound of a hammer clanging on an anvil indicates a blacksmith hard at work making farming tools for the local urban gardeners. Population has declined drastically as most of the region suffered catastrophic droughts and wildfires in conjunction with the economic implosion of bloated industries whose products in

---

[162] See "The Truth About Primitive Life, "in *Technological Slavery* (Port Townsend: Feral House, 2010).

Entertainment and Modern Technology turned out to be far less substantial than the vast reserves of Fossil Fuels upon which they were parasites all along. In the local religious centres, spiritual leaders preach against usury, technological automation, and idling (the sin of working a "job" that involves no real physical labour.) We enter a crowded street market and ask random pedestrians what they think of a world in which seven billion people (an astronomically high figure by the standards of the sparsely populated globe of the far future) spend their entire lives staring at laptop screens and pushing buttons. Will they evaluate this bizarre vision as true? Are their truths about idling, usury, and automation true for them, true eternally, or outright false?

Truth, of course, is an inherently ambiguous term. One is not even sure which register of meaning is implied when one speaks about it. Typically, truth has been thought of as unique to the Gnostic Register of Systems. In Early Analytic Philosophy, this was because truth and falsity were themselves seen as "truth values" within the system of Logic; truth was therefore literally a small subsection of one particular system rather than a general standard which could be applied to the system as a whole, let alone to any of the other four registers. A truth value was considered a result of an operation. If the operation were valid on syntactic grounds, a truth value would result just as trivially as a numerical value would result from a valid arithmetical operation. Under this view, the expression (True & True) yields True just as unproblematically as the expression (2 + 2) yields 4. Likewise, asking about Mythological Truth would be seen as impossible, since the conditions for truth to emerge as a result were inaccessible within that register. Similarly, speaking of memological truth, or sense objective truth, or somatic truth only displayed the ignorance of the person asking after such impossible and nonsensical concepts.

Logical truth is a valid type of truth which can be achieved as a result within the Gnostic Register of meaning through utilizing the resources of some satisfactorily well-defined system but it is only possible from a standpoint grounded in some deeper foundation of Truth. The argument in the present text has been that the Gnostic layer is a legitimate framework of intuition but is

meaningful only to the extent that it implicitly contains the lower orders of meaning. A logical system therefore, however seemingly abstract, is gnostically true only to the extent that it is founded upon sense objective, memological, and somatic truths, but these layers have their own unique requirements for truth which cannot be coerced into the schema of a binary truth value. Instead, there are five headings under which truth can be given, each of which has three modes of truth, falsity, and delusion. These make up 15 modes of truth in total. The present text will conclude therefore with an analysis of each of these but the following table will provide a quick glimpse into how Truth at the somatic layer requires *three*, not two, modes.
[1]

| Heading | Mode | Truth Value | Example |
| --- | --- | --- | --- |
| Veridic | Present | True | Oil exists |
| Veridic | Absent | False | Mammoths are extinct |
| Veridic | Ghost | Delusion | Clean Energy |

Somatic truth occurs within the Veridic Modes of Truth, the criteria used to determine whether the object of an intuition is really "there" or whether one is hallucinating. If the Soma is intended as present and it indeed is present, then the intuition will be true. For example, the intuition in the year 2019 that "Oil exists" is an intuition that passes as true because it instantiates the veridic mode of presence. One can also correctly instantiate the mode of falsity by intending that the Soma is absent. For example, the intuition in the year 2019 that "Woolly mammoths no longer exist" intends a past Soma in its veridic mode of absence. It is important to note, though, that here one correctly discloses falsity, in that the Soma is intended *as absent*. The Soma itself, not the subject's intention of it or statement about it, is therefore revealed to be false. A Soma which is absent is false, just as a Soma that is present is true. Beyond the traditional binary of truth and falsity, though, lies a third option uniquely opened by the author's idiosyncratic redefinition of truth according to veridic modes. One could also intend a Soma as true (present) but find that it is false (absent).

Delusion is the intention of an object that doesn't exist as all, such as the fantasy of a purely Green Soma. The belief that algae will someday be the Soma to power a global cosmopolitan utopia with zero liberal guilt is far worse than false: it is veridically delusional. In other cases, delusion intends an object which once existed but has vanished. The Hindi and Sanskrit word for a ghost भूत (pronounced "Bhoot") demonstrates this concept of finding a ghost where one thought there was life quite well, in that the word "Bhoot" is also the Hindi word for the past, from the Sanrkit word भू ("to be.")[163] Intending a Ghost is therefore not really an act of pure fantasy so much as it is a temporal misrecognition that posits something as present which has already passed over into the past. It is a confusion between Being and what has been. It will be interesting to see how long most people remain within the veridic mode of a ghost intention after Fossil Fuels lose their status as the Soma. The results of this mass delusion are certain to be catastrophic.

This distinction has not gone unnoticed in the body of Peak Oil Literature, though the relation has never obtained the philosophical clarity which the present discussion seeks to achieve. As early as the 2000 *Stormwatch Project*, John Michael Greer warned that many of the factors that made the American middle class lifestyle seem normal during the latter 20th Century will come to an end very soon as a result of Peak Oil; shockingly, he argues that the rest of these factors will not survive this cleansing, since they have *already* disappeared. These past factors misrecognized as present are quite literally ghost factors. A simple dichotomy between presence and absence is therefore quite inadequate to the task of treating the modes by which somatic givenness manifests itself, as there are always three possibilities: presence, absence, and the past ghost.

The memological layer has its own set of modes of truth. In this case, the standard is whether the deep meme is visible to the subject as such. Contrary to expectation, the meme is only true to

---

[163] Pattanaik, Devdutt, *My Hanuman Chalisa* (Rupa Publications: New Delhi, 2017), p. 104.

the extent that it is *not* visible to the subject, for it only emerges as something to be noticed if a problem has occurred in its functioning. Because the criteria is whether it can be seen, these make up the Monstric Modes of Truth, from the Latin word *Monstrare* (to show).
[2]

| Heading | Mode | Truth Value | Example |
|---------|------|-------------|---------|
| Monstric | Invisible | True | David Klass's *Firestorm* |
| Monstric | Visible | False | Initiation into Peak Oil Community |
| Monstric | Alien | Delusion | The modern economist's view on Aristotle, Dante, and Luther |

David Klass's novel *Firestorm* was mentioned near the very beginning of the present text. Although it is a novel about a boy who has been sent from a thousand years in the future to warn about the environmental apocalypse that will follow from our modern industrial lifestyles, he is pursued by villains from the future who try to kill him with ray guns and other super advanced weapons. Of course, the fact that they all have access to a time machine also implies that the future has *even more* technology and energy than we do, despite the fact that we are told it is supposed to be a hellish scenario ravaged by poverty and violence. The deep meme of progress is therefore unquestionably true for David Klass, since it is so pervasive that he can't even see it. The deep meme is true precisely when it is invisible.

On the contrary, a deep meme becomes visible to the subject as an indication of memological breakdown. Those who are initiated into the Peak Oil Community suddenly see the deep meme of progress which had structured their vision before precisely by being invisible. To expose the deep meme in its visibility by explicitly cataloguing the reasons why it can no longer go on providing the memological basis of interpretation is to designate it as false. In a certain sense, this has been the purpose of this entire text. Once again, one's statement *about* the revealed deep meme is not false: the deep meme itself is posited as false.

Finally, a memological difference between a subject's way of thinking and someone else's might be intuited but explained away as an alien mode of thought which some "Other" embodies due to ignorance. Modern fossil fuel-based attitudes towards the past tend to fall into this category. The belief that Dante, Martin Luther, and Aristotle rejected usury simply because of ignorance does not notice the meme in its visibility but it still does notice that a memological difference exists between their beliefs on the issue and the modern economist's. The memological difference is explained away as an "alien" viewpoint deferred onto some archaic and ignorant Other; this only prevents one from having to grasp the somatic and memological reasons why.

[3]

| Heading | Mode | Truth Value | Example |
| --- | --- | --- | --- |
| Sensic | Sense | True | Donkey Cart |
| Sensic | Nonsense | False | Algae-Powered Space Shuttle |
| Sensic | Counter Sense | Delusion | Car |

The sensic modes of truth correlate to the layer of sense objectivity. Sense objects make sense on the basis of their overlap with the deep meme and Soma of an era. A donkey cart embodies the sensic mode of Sense because a donkey cart is a heavy box which must be pulled by a donkey. As a living thing, a donkey can only pull the cart if it is properly fed; this costs a determinate amount of hay and grass from a specific area of land devoted to growing feed, in addition to plenty of drinking water. In addition, the donkey can only spend so many hours per day working; pushing it beyond that limit could kill the donkey and ruin a valuable helper. The donkey cart manifests the truth of the agrarian era.

A space shuttle that runs on algae but can travel to Mars is obviously false; according to the sensic modes of truth, the algae-based space shuttle is not even dignified by the mode of counter sense because there simply is *no* Soma in this intuition. The algae-based space shuttle is a nonsense object. The Clean Energy source powerful enough to enable space travel is not even an intention of fossil fuels in disguise. It is simply a gaze into absence. The subject who intends the algae-based space shuttle in its falsity can intend the truth about its falsity precisely by entering into the sensic mode of nonsense.

On the contrary, a car is a counter sense object. An airport shuttle service can run a van 24 hours per day with revolving employees who require more rest than the car itself. Fuel is empirically limited but is felt to be an infinite source available at the pump down the street at all times and for a reasonable price. The vehicle requires no labour to operate and can transport a full load of people remarkably vast distances in a short period of time. A car is a vehicle that accomplishes a sublime amount of work for a person who is spared from doing any work in the process, which runs on a frighteningly finite resource which is misrecognized to be infinite. Ordinarily, if the subject embodies the deep meme of progress to a level invisible to himself or herself, this counter sense will not be recognized as such because the fossil fuels which underlie it will allow the user to keep insisting that, at the very least, it isn't false because its existence can be empirically confirmed quite easily. The counter sense object is delusion embodied

The gnostic modes of truth are the modes by which individual values within a system are evaluated as true, false, or delusional. Because the gnostic layer is populated by systematic values rather than tangible objects, the gnostic modes of truth require a brief analysis of Edmund Husserl's early work *The Philosophy of Arithmetic*. Husserl's earliest work reflected his background as a Mathematician interested in the veridic status of impossible mathematical values, specifically, the imaginary number *i* (the square root of -1). [164] The square root of -1 is a strange value because even though one cannot represent it more literally than with the letter *i*, one can still derive arithmetically-valid results through

---

[164] Husserl, Edmund, *The Philosophy of Arithmetic* (Dordrecht: Kluwer Academic Publishers, 2003), p. liv.

submitting it to calculation. For example, because one already knows that $i^2 = -1$, one can find through simple calculation that $i^3 = -i$ and $i^4 = 1$. Rising to higher powers will restart the cycle by circulating through a finite set of predictable values, each of which was obtained on perfectly legitimate arithmetical grounds.

The only difficulty, of course, is that we cannot have any clearer intuition of what $i$ is in itself. Husserl therefore questioned whether $i$ differed from the ordinary counting numbers such as 3, 6, and 10. The counting numbers could be given as "authentically representable multiplicities."[165] For example, if one had an intuition of three apples, one had an authentic relation to the number 3 because one could grasp the number intuitively. But for numbers larger than 10, this authentic relation would break down. Even if one did see 1,234 fava beans in an intuition, one would not be able to grasp the number 1,234 intuitively. One could still, however, relate to this number through a symbol. The inscription "1,234" certainly does allow a path of access to the number by providing a symbolic pathway for consciousness to reach it: like electricity, intentionality will travel a long distance to reach its object, provided it has reasonable conduction along the way.[166] The imaginary number $i$, however, differs in that the problem is not that it is too large to be grasped except symbolically: the problem is there is no value which could be given authentically, even provided one's ceiling for intuitive grasp were raised to a sublimely high level. In summary, the number 3 is authentically given to intuition. The number 1,234 is given signitively (through a sign) to intuition. The number $i$ is given only as imaginary.

The author will borrow Husserl's terminology to describe the three modes of gnostic truth. However, the author will expand the range of interest far beyond that of numbers to include all gnostic contents. The following table situates them in relation to truth, falsity, and delusion:
[4]

| Heading | Mode | Truth Value | Example |
| --- | --- | --- | --- |

---

[165] Ibid., p. 16.
[166] Ibid., p. xlvii.

| Gnostic | Intuitive | True | 3 |
| Gnostic | Signitive | False | Kurzweil's Immortality Algorithm |
| Gnostic | Imaginary | Delusional | Extant Computing Constructs |

No doubt, some gnostic values can be given authentically to intuition. In this case, the object is more or less grasped in its own presence rather than reconstructed at the end of a symbolic process of calculation or posited as completely hypothetical. One does not have to have a complete grasp of an entity for it to still qualify as a genuine gnostic essence which can be verified in rational consciousness. It makes no difference, for example, whether the number 3 is "really" a logical class of all triplets (Russell), the extension of a concept (Frege), an innate idea of the Cogito (Descartes), or an eternal Idea (Plato). Knowing the ultimate ontological status of 3 is not necessary to know that it is a genuine gnostic essence which can be made "present" to consciousness in an act of transcendent penetration into something which really has Being.

On the contrary, some gnostic values are posited on *purely signitive grounds* and lack any intuitive confirmation whatsoever. For example, Ray Kurzweil claims that exponential increases in computing power can be extrapolated into the future to predict that someday soon the machines will be artificially intelligent enough to invent machines which are smarter enough than their parent machines to solve previously unsolvable problems, even including death. Of course, the "immortality algorithm" is here posited as a gnostic essence which could ideally be mapped into a set of familiar mathematical symbols. One should distinguish, however, the symbols of which it would be composed from the algorithm itself. Clearly, appealing to "mathematical rigour" to justify the presumed existence of something as blatantly ridiculous as an algorithm to cure death will not overcome the simple fact that what one is speaking about simply does not exist and never will. Providing a gnostic symbol is not enough: there must be some viable pathway, however abstract, to travel from the sign to the essence it represents. Kurzweil's Immortality Algorithm is falsity and absence embodied in a gnostic medium.

On the other hand, there are some systematic contents which are misread as autonomous entities with independent existence but are really just ephemeral euphemisms whose basis of existence is fading away as the author writes these words. Computing constructs such as "list comprehension," "struct," "void pointer," or "array of doubles" might superficially seem to be the same kind of gnostic essences as the traditional numbers such as 3 or 15. In reality, one is guilty of equivocation if one does not expose how even the word "system" has an idiosyncratic meaning in this context. One might say that in the Ancient and Medieval eras, one dealt with Metaphysical Systems and that from Kant to the early 20th Century one dealt with Transcendental Systems. Increasingly in our era, we are not even dealing with either. Our systems are mostly just Executable Systems. In this case, the system has no fixed existence in the things themselves (the Metaphysical View) or even in the subject's purified faculties (the Transcendental View.) The system exists only so long as it is in a state of execution. What this means more literally is that the system only exists as long as some piece of hardware burns electricity. The highest truth about the system, therefore, is just the empirical observation that "electricity is being consumed over there." The Imaginary gnostic mode of truth describes constructs which have no independent existence but are only achievable as secondary results of burning fossil fuels. Like Husserl's understanding of the Imaginary Number $i$, there is no literal inscription of the content in itself. It can only be read secondarily from the processes in which it is involved. To ask the question, "What is a struct in itself without the process of electricity consumption?" is to search for an entity which simply does not exist in itself. Misreading these ghost essences as enduring, independent, present substances might be called veridicization: one mistakes a super high level side effect of the Soma for the Soma itself. Our era is the era of the Ghost.

Finally, the Credic modes of truth correlate to the register of Mythology. In this case, the criteria of truth is the extent to which a

myth is believed ("Credic" is the author's own term derived from the Latin term "credere."). The Credic modes of truth determine whether a mythological event that has been disclosed is tacitly evaluated as denoting some real presence, whether it offers a glimpse into a historic past whose absence is registered as such, or whether it presents the impossible in the guise of Truth. The Following table will synopsize these results:
[5]

| Heading | Mode | Example |
| --- | --- | --- |
| Credic | Believed | South Korea's Technological Modernization |
| Credic | Impossible | Elon Musk's Voyage to Mars |
| Credic | Historical | Modern Catholic attitudes toward Medieval status of Usury as Mortal Sin |

The Credic mode of believed mythology is paradoxical, in that through it one accepts a mythological event precisely by failing to see that it is a mythological event. The Modern American belief that they are the only culture with no myths stems from the simple fact that the Mythology of Progress is so unproblematically and so thoughtlessly accepted by them that they fail to even see it as such. Even if one were to interrogate such a person about progress, he or she would likely insist that it doesn't count as a myth: it is simply "objective reality" and "scientific fact."

On the other hand, some myths are presented through the second Credic mode of impossibility. Any minimally rational subject should be smart enough to realize that Elon Musk's plan to travel to Mars is impossible for geological reasons alone: there are not enough Fossil Fuels to provide the raw energy to colonize the planet Mars. Further, even if a journey were somehow made to that planet, the passengers would suffer radioactive poisoning which would easily defeat the purpose of "leaving the Earth to seek a better life." It is arguable that even Mr. Musk himself does not really believe that this is an event which could really take place. In one speech he claimed that his motivation to colonize Mars was just to be able to wake up in the morning and feel that life still had a purpose. After achieving billionaire status, Musk apparently found that even with abundant money, he still needed something to do with all of his time. Kaczynski's warning that even the wealthiest people still need to go through the Power Process seems to be the real truth behind this Mythology which is clearly meant to be presented in the impossible Credic mode even to those who claim to take it seriously.

Finally, the third Credic mode of historical mythology presents an event as something that certainly could have happened in the past but would not be conceivable in the present. For example, few Roman Catholics today even know that usury was once a major item on the list of mortal sins. As was mentioned earlier in the present work, it is not a coincidence that Dante, Martin Luther, St. John Chrysostom, and the anonymous author of the *Apocalypse of Peter* all listed usury as a damnable offense (in other words, the consequence of usury was *literally* Hell.) If interrogated about this, most practicing Roman Catholics would likely dismiss this fact as "historical truth." Though they probably could not articulate *why* someone who practiced usury in the year 900 AD is still in Hell today for it but someone who practiced usury in the year 1994 is not, they would have the sense that even the teachings of the Catholic Church on Mortal Sin can lose their truth value with the passage of time. Interestingly, this loss of Truth was not due to a disappearance of the literal texts which once embodied it. The Vatican certainly still has all of the medieval documents condemning usurers to eternal punishment, yet even with the exact same syntactic structure preserved intact the same string of words will have lost its Truth by losing a Presence that once animated it as something more living than a dead historical relic. Bertrand Russell's and Gottlob Frege's search for the eternally-valid syntactic requirements of Truth as a gnostic system of Logic therefore cannot account for a loss of Truth with no syntactic explanation.

Many of the people who dabble in Neo-Pagan ritual would likely respond the same way if asked whether it were possible to restore the cults of *every* pagan god in the Ancient World. While they would likely acknowledge that the religion of an obscure Ram God in an extinct Near Eastern Civilization was true at the time when it was taken seriously by a whole community of people for whom its rituals, sacrifices, and chants were a part of daily life, it is no longer true and cannot be revived.

There is a tacit sense that a truth has "lost its presence," even if all of its information is still intact. What few will realize is that this Presence which animated Truth in one era but vanished in the next is the Soma. The truths we take for granted as eternally valid today will go the way of usury in the Roman Catholic Church or pagan gods in extinct ancient religions. Certainly, someone *could* discover a snippet of the Google Algorithm in the year 2340, although it is doubtful how many non-electronic copies will have been recorded that could survive to the 24th Century. But even if one had the syntactic or symbolic information exactly right, it will be untrue in a world in which gigantic data centres will no longer burn sublime amounts of electrical energy to power a 24/7, globally-connected extravaganza of mindless entertainment to billions of users. One will find, instead, that Truth is, at its deepest level, just Presence and that the Soma was never a fixed entity which could be counted upon to last forever. The Soma has a fragile, temporary existence which only lasts as long as its physical reserves are not depleted into oblivion. The following table synopsizes all of the modes of Truth:
[6]

| Modes of Truth | Criteria | Members |
|---|---|---|
| Veridic | Modes of Somatic Givenness | • Present<br>• Absent<br>• Ghost |
| Monstric | Modes of | • Invisible |

|  | Visibility of Shape | • Visible<br>• Alien |
|---|---|---|
| Sensic | Modes of Sense Object | • Sense<br>• Nonsense<br>• Counter Sense |
| Gnostic | Modes of Value | • Intuitive<br>• Signitive<br>• Imaginary |
| Credic | Modes of Credibility of Mythic Event | • Believed<br>• Impossible<br>• Historic |

*Other Possible Hierarchies of Meaning*

In conclusion, it is important to emphasize that the author's decision to locate Soma at the deepest layer of the hierarchy should not be misread as a Materialist statement such as, "There is no horizon of meaning whatsoever outside of the particular hierarchy dominated by the Soma." Soma occupies the deepest position of the hierarchy available to human subjects only because human subjects are literally limited by their survival needs as earthly beings who can only continue to live through hunting and gathering, agrarian farming, fossil fuel industrialism, or through post-industrial salvage. This does not mean that somatic essences are the only type of essences that exist or that could exist. In fact, even within the hierarchy of five layers dominated by the Soma, each of the four higher order layers offers a vague window into non-somatic essences and non-somatic truths.

For example, the author does not mean to imply that spiritual essences don't exist simply because they are not somatic in nature. Rather, it is perfectly rational to accept that pneumatic essences (to use the author's own term borrowed from πνεῦμα the Ancient Greek word for spirit) denote entities with an independent or real existence, even if they are intrinsically not of a somatic nature and can only be viewed partially and imperfectly within the subject's horizon of meaning. Pneumatic essences' lack of full clarity do not indicate a lack of real existence; the difficulty simply stems from the fact that the subject's hierarchy of meanings is grounded in the Soma and carries this somatic substance into each layer regardless of whether it is recognized or not.

John Michael Greer's theory of the Planes of Being is helpful for considering a distinction of types; within this list, the Soma can be recognized to be only one of several kinds of transcendent essence. Although John Michael Greer is not a Phenomenologist, one can still find faint echoes of a Material Ontology in his Planes of Being in *Mystery Teachings from the Living Earth*. Readers new to Greer may be shocked when perusing his list of publications to find a nearly equal proportion between works about the serious material problem of fossil fuel depletion and works about the mysterious spiritual subject of magic. The two cannot, however, be divorced without losing the integrity of Greer's holistic thought. As a practicing mage and druid, he has explained the rationale behind Druidry as the need to break from the false dichotomy of spiritless scientific materialism and materially-ignorant New Age spiritualism. Both, ironically enough, are equally inhibitive of a serious response to Peak Oil. While the New Age idealist would argue that material problems are really spiritual problems in disguise, the spiritless scientific materialist would argue that spiritual problems are really material problems in disguise. Consider, for example, the idea that the appropriate response to encountering hard material limits in Peak Oil is to devote considerable spiritual exercise to the task of wishing them out of existence. This approach would be just as misguided as the scientific materialist's decision to ignore spiritual motivations and to instead just turn to drugging the population until they are biochemically forced to comply with a spiritual change they did not agree to by choice. The more likely outcome in either case is for a material response to remain stuck at the level of material being and for a spiritual response to remain stuck at the level of spiritual being. Each may perhaps accomplish an impressive amount in its own realm, but no matter how large its influence there might be, it will never be enough to turn a quantitative leap in its own realm into a qualitative leap out of its own region into another which it did not deserve to enter.

There is, of course, one notable exception to this impossibility of leaping out of or across regions: that exception is Magic. Magic, for Greer is simply the science of using willed changes in consciousness to pursue paths of influence between material and spiritual planes of being which are otherwise devoid of contact. The fact that consciousness is something of a unique region of being in itself, neither material nor spiritual per se but a point of intersection allowing legitimate pathways of mutual contact, is a testament to the viability of Greer's Ontology of the Planes of Being; one might even consider this to be something of a Material Ontology of regional stratification reminiscent of Husserlian Phenomenology.[167] At any rate, one is guilty of a logical error of equivocation if one uses the word "being" indiscriminately to refer to material essences and to refer to spiritual essences without regard for the way that the being of each differs in a way that admits of no common ground.

Greer was not the only major recent thinker to recognize that pneumatic essences must be taken seriously as legitimate types of phenomena rather than written off as superstitions upheld by the "ignorant." In a previously-unreleased "Letter to M. K.", Ted Kaczynski recounts a fascinating episode from his early life in which he hiked through a stretch of forest so unspoiled by industrial activity that he could drink from the stream without boiling the water first. Yet this site's natural integrity was not to endure for much longer: already, signs of construction crews were emerging to transform this land into just another stretch of highway to be lined with modern houses and shops. He did not react to the destruction

---

[167] In *Ideas*, Husserl argued that there were multiple regions of Material Ontology with no single universal genus under which they could all be fit. A spatial temporal physical object, for example, could not be fit into the same genus as a psychic act or the region of pure consciousness because the minimal transcendental features of each were incompatible. A spatial temporal object has the essence of requiring to be given in a series of partial perspectives but psychic acts and consciousness itself are not bound by such a requirement because they have different essences and are from different regions.

of this natural site as *simply* the destruction of some natural physical essence, however:

> I stopped and said a kind of prayer to the spirit of the spring. It was a prayer in which I swore that I would take revenge for what was being done to the forest . . . and then I returned home as quickly as I could because- I have something to do! You can guess what it was.[168]

In a rare interview conducted after his imprisonment, Kaczynski was asked to narrate a typical day in his life in the woods. He responded by recounting hunting rabbits for meat but mentioned that he would always thank the rabbit after it had been ethically hunted by saying a prayer for the "demi-god Grandfather Rabbit."[169] One should not interpret these references to the "spirit of the spring" and "Grandfather Rabbit" as some metaphorical descriptions of somatic essences any more than one should interpret Greer's references to spiritual phenomena which are stimulated to activity in magical ritual to be a metaphor for some reductively material object. Although strict censorship within the privileged halls of the academy would make such a discussion impossible, it is simply intellectually dishonest to ignore that Greer's and Kaczynski's positions as radical outliers to the official academic presses allowed them the freedom to acknowledge a distinction between spirit and matter which would be impossible to formulate within the confines of academic prejudice. Similarly, to argue that a pneumatic spiritual phenomena does not obey the transcendental structural requirements of a somatic physical body does not at all refute its existence: it merely states the fact that the two manifest themselves unto consciousness through irreconcilable structures, which was precisely the point of treating them as different types of essences in the first place.

---

[168] Ted Kaczynski, "Letter to M.K.", p. 375
[169] Kaczynski mentions his ritual of thanking the demi-god Grandfather Rabbit in "An Interview with Ted" in *Technological Slavery* (Port Townsend: Feral House, 2010), p. 400.

Because the subject is a finite, physical entity whose existence depends upon the continued presence of the Soma and the continued manifestation of the limited Apocalypse, things can only appear as meaningful within a horizon of somatic limitation. This is not because *nothing* exists at all except the Soma, as though spirits were just ideological reflections of matter or some Marxist cliché. Rather, it is because the subject is inherently limited by finitude that transcendent spiritual essences can only manifest themselves according to the terms established within a hierarchy that carries the Soma up into each higher order layer.

Likewise, it is not that pneumatic essences cannot manifest themselves at all: it is rather that they can only do so within the frame of Mythology (as conditioned by a particular way of life for a people grounded in history and the Soma.) It is not a coincidence that even the most abstract spiritual truths can only make sense when situated into a mythic event. To say that Lord Shiva is nothing because the phrase "Shi-va" literally means "that which is not" in Sanskrit is a profound but extremely vague spiritual insight: but the mythic image of Shiva sitting still in silent meditation for months provides its proper horizon of Phenomenological fulfilment.[170] Even though a spiritual essence may have an autonomous existence, it is unknowable to the subject except through its disclosure in a mythic event. Likewise, the mythological events of the *Iliad* are not a trivial supplement beyond the abstract truths about the Greek Gods: the "purified truths" about the Gods are themselves just abstractions from the mythic events in which this knowledge ultimately originated. Similarly, Paul may be the New Testament writer whose lack of knowledge about the empirical details of Jesus' biography is outdone only by the writer of James, yet his knowledge of even just a few significant events such as the crucifixion and resurrection provided the narratological basis from which he devised one of the most sophisticated abstract theologies of all time.

In addition to the Mythological Layer's ability to provide partial insight into independent pneumatic essences, the Systematic

---

[170] Sadghuru, *Adiyogi: The Source of Yoga* (Noida: HarperCollins, 2017), p. 28. Murty, Sudha, "The Indian Cupid", in *The Man from the Egg: Unusual Tales about the Trinity* (Gurgaon: Penguib, 2017), p. 25.

Layer is a legitimate window by which the subject can penetrate towards transcendent gnostic essences. The number 3 is not an ideological distortion of class struggle: it is a legitimate gnostic essence which must be respected as an autonomous entity. Above all else, the subject should react with *gratitude* that this window is open, if only incompletely. Still, although it does make sense to consider the number 3 to be an autonomous gnostic essence which could endure in its existence even if there were no human subjects to contemplate it, it can only even be *partially* revealed to human subjects through some gnostic system. Even the most primitive act of counting from one to ten with one's fingers is still a gnostic system of abstract values distinguished by rank. On the other hand, even the most sophisticated Mathematical system will still be ultimately inconclusive as a system, even if it does provide a glimpse into a Mathematical entity like 3 which can be accepted as "real" rather than an idealistic illusion. Even systems which are incompatible with one another at the level of fundamentals can still provide equally legitimate pathways to penetrate into the transcendent essence of particular abstract entities. It does not matter that Plato, Descartes, Frege, and Russell disagree on something as basic as the definition of number. Plato considered numbers to be permanent Ideas in a World of Forms; Descartes considered numbers to be innate ideas which the Cogito got access to for free; Frege considered numbers to be extensions of concepts; Russell considered numbers to be higher order classes of classes.[171] But each one still provided a valid pathway of exploration for the subject to touch, however incompletely, the transcendent gnostic object of a 3.

  The inconclusiveness of individual systems leads to a proliferation of many incompatible systems which all still lay claim to, at the very least, an incomplete intuition of an abstract truth which can be accepted to endure independently of any of them. The author's own view is that because a transcendent mathematical essence like 3 can only be revealed to the subject within the gnostic register of meaning, this can only be accomplished through

---

[171]For Russell, the number one is the class of all singletons; the number two is the class of all pairs; the number three is the class of trios etc.

adopting some system of abstract values ordered by rank. Yet precisely because "rank" is a transcendental requirement of meaning, the system itself will rest upon a perpetually insecure foundation no matter how secure the particular entities it might open an incomplete pathway to view might be.

This is, however, itself just a result of the fact that the hierarchy of meanings is grounded in the Soma. It is not that each layer only presents materialist reflections of the same Soma in a different mode, which would be the Marxist view. It is rather that even if one does penetrate beyond the Soma and beyond one's own limited field of vision to tangentially touch an abstract essence with no intrinsically somatic features, one can only do so within a layer of meaning which is founded upon the Soma. The systems of Plato, Descartes, Frege, and Russell are incomplete for the same reason: they are formulated within a hierarchy grounded in a Soma and mediated by memological and counter sense objective influences which twist even the purest intentions to fit a certain shape. The Soma is not the Marxist Material Base because it is not the sole type of entity which could exist: it is, rather, the substance upon which even our most carefully-executed explorations of non-somatic abstractions must take place. The Soma is a testament to the subject's existentialist finitude, since as a subject constrained by the transcendental conditions of appearance, the subject cannot short-circuit these limitations to directly gaze into non-somatic truths but must instead find pathways by which they can bring themselves to Apocalyptic manifestation within a fragile hierarchy grounded in Soma.

Likewise, there is no theoretical contradiction between the author's portrayal of a hierarchy of layers of meaning grounded in Soma in the present text and the idea that other hierarchies of meaning could exist that do not take Soma as their basis. Speaking about subjective awareness outside somatic context is also theoretically possible. A hierarchy of meaning grounded purely in mentatic awareness is certainly a theoretical possibility and this is arguably what Thomas Aquinas and Abu-Nasr Al Farabi envisioned God, as the supreme abstract intellect, to be in the Middle Ages. A hierarchy grounded in the gnostic is also theoretically possible, in which case one would find Plato's theory of a World of Forms in which purified gnostic intelligences gaze at the autonomous truths without the limitations of a somatically-grounded transcendental filter. Or perhaps even a hierarchy grounded in a purified Pneumatic base, in which case the old Pagan notion of a plurality of spiritual gods, each of whom has purely pneumatic consciousness, might be the result.

*Isomorphisms: Transcendent, Transcendental, Imminent*

The only thing which is absolutely certain to the author is that none of these horizons is the one that we as finite human subjects have to work within. For us, the best we can hope for is a minimally acceptable isomorphism between what really exists and what manifests itself to us. We cannot seize a gnostic essence like a 3 and take it hostage, nor can we contemplate Lord Shiva or Jesus Christ or even Zeus outside the frame of mythology, but we can recognize the ways in which Truth itself is given to us. This requires that some schema of isomorphism can be trusted to present a truth from a transcendent region in a form which is intelligible in a hierarchy grounded in the Soma. In other words, Truth hinges on a promise of isomorphism.

Earlier in the present text, the classic example of isomorphism was already mentioned: Descartes discovered that an ordered pair of numbers can represent a location on a graph and that a location on a graph can represent an ordered pair of numbers. The same meaning, in other words, could be represented either way. Whereas one typically would think that the philosophical question of interest is which of the two is the origin and which is the copy, the author would suggest that this question is inherently mistaken: a tuple of numbers such as (2,4) and the location on a graph which it represents are *both* copies of the same gnostic essence which is irreducible to either. This is because both of them are indigenous to some gnostic system of meaning and compatible with the requirements of apocalyptic manifestation unique to a subject's Phenomenological horizon. It can be granted that there is "something" on the other side which really exists as a purified gnostic essence. But as soon as some revelation of it is achieved in the medium of gnostic rationality, the essence itself has been lost in favour of a systematic value. The best we can hope for is to achieve an isomorphism to it, however partial. Similarly, Euclid's *Elements*, an Ancient system long since considered disproven, remains even to this day a very incomplete glimpse into the truths of Geometry, because it provides an isomorphic window, however partial, into some transcendent gnostic truths. There really is "something on the other side." The same could be argued about Isaac Newton's and Galileo's similarly outdated insights into Physics. Despite an obvious incompleteness and imperfection, it would be absurd to say that there's "nothing on the other side" of their theories: partiality does not negate a transcendent isomorphism because what is transcendent to it can only be glimpsed imperfectly to a subject whose frame of intuition is limited by somatic finitude.

Transcendent isomorphism is not, however, the only kind of isomorphism. In addition, one might argue that the present text has been all about the transcendental isomorphism that holds between different layers of the hierarchy of meanings. The Mythology of the American Dream is not isomorphic to a transcendent mathematical truth but it is still accepted as true because of its transcendental isomorphism to the Soma and to the intermediary layers which lay between the two. Transcendental isomorphisms are intrinsically less accountable than transcendent essences because the standard of truth is simply measured with the circular reasoning of whether a mythological content accords with a memological content which itself accords with the Soma (all of which were already in the subject.) Yet transcendental isomorphisms are nonetheless perfectly legitimate standards of truth. They are however far more fragile than transcendent isomorphisms because mere historical contingency sustains them in their truth.

The final type of isomorphism is of course the imminent but it is also the weakest and the most deceptive. A transcendent isomorphism is inherently constrained by the transcendent essence it seeks to provide a window of truth into: one does not create the object (such as a Euclidian circle or a Cartesian coordinate system) or even manipulate it at will. A transcendental isomorphism is also constrained by being grounded in the Soma which must exist and must maintain its presence to prevent its hierarchy of higher level truths from dissolving into falsity. An imminent isomorphism, however, has no need to penetrate to a transcendent essence on the outside or even to maintain respect for the transcendental structures of subjective meaning: an imminent isomorphism simply reduplicates a content from within by repeating it in a superficially distinct form which bears no essential distinction from its origin and is unconstrained with regard to *how* it accomplishes this arbitrary repetition. For example, computers cheat around their inherent lack of language by mapping a sub-system of pseudo-linguistic character symbols to a sub-system of pseudo-numerical values on a one to one basis. In the classic example, the integer value 97 is reliably mapped to the alphabetical symbol 'a' but the isomorphism between 97 and 'a' was not discovered through a transcendent penetration into an exterior mathematical truth (Euclid) or even a transcendent physical truth (Galileo.) Two values were simply paired on an ad hoc basis. Yet even the number 97 can hardly be considered to be an a priori origin which was rationally "discovered" as already existing. This number was itself isomorphically fitted to the electrical state correlated to the binary signature 01100001. At its deepest level, neither the alphabetical character 'a' nor the number 97 are "really in the machine" as objective entities that were discovered. One only obtains a set of pseudo-linguistic symbols through providing a contrived imminent isomorphism to a set of integer values which were themselves obtained through the contrived isomorphism to a set of electronic states.

  Because of this completely artificial character, this process has no protection against falling into infinite recursion. After correlating the electronic state 01100001 to the pseudo-number 97 which was then correlated to the pseudo-linguistic symbol 'a,' one could go on to correlate 'a' to the truth value 'true.' To think that truth has been reduced to the fourth remove from an empirical act of burning electricity in a machine is a testament to the degraded status truth has fallen into in our era. It is frightening that imminent isomorphism is quickly coming to eclipse any other standard of truth. Whereas Galileo and Isaac Newton were legitimately interested in achieving transcendent penetration to eternal truths which had an independent, autonomous existence, the "top geniuses" of our era seem to have lost even the notion that there could be a set of transcendent truths which were not arbitrarily mapped from one set of data values to another as a result of some engineer's ad hoc design. There is a disturbing sense in which imminent isomorphism allows a company to literally "create the truth" by engineering a sub-system of redundancies over an established system over which they own the intellectual property rights. Somewhere along the way, the subject itself will vanish, as the very need to go beyond itself to discover truth will have long since been replaced by an impersonal set of operations which unfolded within the secrecy and darkness of a machine completely devoid of subjectivity anyway. The subject's immersion in the pixel screen illusions that radiate from a screen ultimately beholden to a remote location the user cannot even intend Phenomenologically will surely lead to a type of subjective death. Yet even before this ghastly outcome arises, the Soma which provided the sole basis for this madness will have been depleted out of existence, collapsing entire worlds of Truth into meaninglessness and falsity in the process.

The first volume of the work *Being and Oil* likewise will conclude on this note. It is the author's hope that this volume provided a glimpse into the theoretical problems of an Ontology of Limitation, a Phenomenology of Transcendental Meaning, and a Philosophy of Truth which was satisfactorily clear to enable a discussion of issues considered to lie within the realm of Practical Philosophy. The second volume of *Being and Oil* will continue this discussion by formulating a Peak Oil Philosophy of Ethics, Politics, and Religion that transcend traditional political binaries which have thus far stifled meaningful response to the unfolding crisis of Peak Oil. In addition, the second volume shall provide a detailed analysis of the coming crises which will disrupt ordinary life on the planet Earth over the course of the 21$^{st}$ Century as the Soma fades into absence and a new world emerges in its place.

Printed in Great Britain
by Amazon